Mind Maps for
Effective Project Management

Mind Maps for
Effective Project Management

Maneesh Dutt

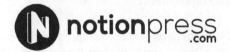

Notion Press

5 Muthu Kalathy Street, Triplicane,

Chennai - 600 005

First Published by Notion Press 2015

Copyright © Maneesh Dutt 2015

All Rights Reserved.

ISBN: 978-93-52060-44-3

Cataloging in Publication Data--DK
Courtesy: D.K. Agencies (P) Ltd. <docinfo@dkagencies.com>
Dutt, Maneesh, 1970- **author.**
Mind maps for effective project management/Maneesh Dutt.   pages cm   Includes bibliographical references.   ISBN 9789352060443
1. Project management.   2. Brain mapping.   3. Thought and thinking.   I. Title.
HD69.P75D88 2015   DDC 658.404   23

Dedicated to

My parents

My teachers

All Mind Mappers

and

Project Teams across the globe

Acknowledgement

My journey with Mind Maps began with the book "*How to Mind Map*" by Tony Buzan [1]. This little book altered my thinking completely. And for this, I will remain eternally grateful to Mr. Tony Buzan. Further experimentations with Mind Maps gave me the confidence to synergize my twin passions of Mind Mapping and Project Management in the form of this book.

I would like to extend my heartfelt thanks to Chris Griffith for writing the Foreword for my book. His life and his book "*GRASP the Solution*" [2] continue to inspire me to discover new frontiers in Mind Mapping.

My sincere thanks to all the authors mentioned in the bibliography without whom this book would not have been possible. A special thanks to the Project Management Institute for its flagship publication "*Project Management Body of Knowledge*" i.e. *PMBOK* [3], which provided the reference framework for designing many of the Mind Maps in this book.

This book would not have been possible without all the Mind Mappers and project managers across the globe, whose countless articles and discussion fora motivated me to take the plunge and embark on my journey of Mind Maps.

I would like to convey my gratitude to all my friends for giving me the encouragement to follow my heart and pursue my interest in Mind Mapping. This is indeed invaluable for a first time book author.

I would like to acknowledge Aparna Sharma for her deep and thorough editing of the second edition of this book. This has not only given a new lease of life to it but also clearly reinforced the core messages being communicated in this book.

I am also indebted to my good friend Manoj Kumar, who painstakingly reviewed the book removing many an unseen error and ensured a consistency in messages. His valuable feedback urged me to take a relook at the book both from a Project Management reader's perspective and that of enthusiastic Mind Map readers.

A hearty thanks to my close friend, Ganesh, for letting in his basement office (away from mobile networks and my little energetic twins Kaamya and Krish) to afford me the much desired peace while working to give the book its final shape.

And, of course, Notion Press deserves a special mention for leveraging their experience and getting the book ready for wide audiences across the globe.

Most importantly, I would like to highlight the huge contribution made by my wife Seema, who not only helped me with the Mind Map templates in this book but her overall support indeed has been critical in helping it see the light of day.

Contents

Mind Map Illustrations and Templates Included in this Book

Foreword by Chris Griffiths

Most business processes, including the project management of products and services, are dying for a shake-up. Relying on your old methods of doing things will get you nowhere – just because they worked for you in the past certainly doesn't mean that they will bring you success this time around. Mind Mapping is an infinitely versatile tool that will breathe new life into stuffy business operations and overhaul the way you manage your products forever.

This book provides an extensive, in-depth guide into Mind Mapping and how it can be applied to project management to unleash your full creative power, drive innovation throughout your team and in turn sky-rocket your organization's growth.

Maneesh was first introduced to me a few years ago when he attended one of ThinkBuzan's training courses. He became a ThinkBuzan Licensed Instructor in Mind Mapping and iMindMap, having been trained and accredited by the inventor of Mind Maps himself, Tony

Buzan. I highly respect Maneesh as a trainer, for setting out to help others enhance their creativity, and for taking the risk and quitting his previous job to be able to do so in the first place. This commitment and passion for Mind Mapping, creativity and innovation is echoed throughout this book.

With his wealth of experience and knowledge in the fields of Mind Mapping and project management, Maneesh has cemented himself as a thought leader. In this book, he will show you how Mind Mapping can improve key project management skills, how you can boost your creativity when it comes to the project creation and management, and how Mind Mapping can be used at every stage of a project for utmost effectiveness.

These days, Mind Maps are being used broadly within organizations to aid the management of projects. You will be amazed at how, through Mind Mapping, you can streamline and organize your projects and approach them with creativity and flair.

Chris Griffiths

Founder and CEO of OpenGenius, the parent company of ThinkBuzan, creators of the iMindMap software and ThinkProductivity, creators of DropTask

Best-selling author, GRASP The Solution

Penarth, Wales

Introduction

"Good Project Management practices need to ensure that there are no loose ends anywhere. And with Mind Maps there never can be any since they are designed to connect."

It was sometime in 2009 during a routine 9-5 job that I was moving from one meeting room to another frenetically chasing schedules. As I settled into an empty conference room waiting for others to join in, I saw a book lying on the table with the cover facing down. Being fond of books and reading, I instinctively picked it up, little knowing that this 6" x 6" book would kick-start a new phase in my life. The book was *"How to Mind Map"* by Tony Buzan [1]. The book looked interesting and while waiting for the others to join, I started reading it. Little did I realise that over the next two hours or so I had finished reading the book. Luckily for me nobody had come to disturb in and eventually the only meeting that happened was between me and this book. Excited and curious I bought three books on the subject the same evening and my Mind Mapping journey began.

I started experimenting with the concept first myself, subsequently with my kids, and soon started applying Mind Maps actively in my organisation in a variety of situations. Each instance I was amazed with the kind of results I was getting using this deceptively simple but unusually powerful tool. One thing led to another and the crowning achievement for me was the formal learning of this very powerful concept from the man himself, Tony Buzan, the inventor of Mind Maps. This finally gave me the confidence to quit my job and commit myself wholeheartedly to the subject of Mind Mapping and further realising its full potential.

As a freelancer I started meeting senior management and heads of organisations to introduce Mind Mapping into organisations. And I was pleasantly surprised by a common reaction from many of these very senior people, which roughly boils down to: "I have been using Mind Maps very effectively for developing my top level strategies but....am not sure how my organisation, my teams could use it further?" Realizing that a majority of organisations work on a wide variety of projects I decided to fill up this need through this book. In effect, this is a humble attempt to arrange a marriage between the two subjects: Project Management and Mind Mapping my twin passions in life!!

So I started by asking a fundamental question: is managing projects fun and engaging?

It certainly does not seem so, going by a joint study by McKinsey & Company and University of Oxford [4], of 5400 large Scale IT Projects, indicates that only 55% of these projects were actually delivered within budgets. Though there are a variety of reasons for project delays and cost overruns but no one can deny that a project headed towards failure could do a lot better with an added ounce of creativity. Any project, which falls short of meeting customer requirements reflects a lack of creativity while managing projects.

It is an interesting paradox that the process of creation, of any product or service (i.e. any project), itself suffers or can suffer from a lack of creativity!

Moreover, the general image of a project manager is usually that of a stressed individual pushing his team to meet client deadlines working under various constraints. In this scenario, is it possible to introduce an element of fun and hence creativity in projects?

After completing his daily grind, a project manager heads for the soccer field to relieve himself of the tensions of the day. Despite an intense game of soccer he feels refreshed and wonders why after burning so many calories he feels invigorated whereas after office hours he feels sapped of energy without burning as many calories? The difference is due to the fact that office is equated with "work time" whereas soccer represents "play time". Interestingly, the more we are involved in an activity, the less it feels like work. Put another way, our level of engagement with an activity defines whether our mind equates it with "work" or "play". So the moot question is: can projects be made more engaging? Decades of "standard" project management practices are giving way to a definite movement towards making project management practices more engaging. Techniques such as Agile have started to introduce an essence of fun into projects. But is that enough?

Now let's look at what is a Mind Map.

A Mind Map is a simple tool directed to enhance our engagement in an activity thus propelling us into a zone of enhanced creativity. We are at our creative best when we immerse ourselves fully into a task oblivious of our surroundings. All of us have experienced these moments say while painting, dancing, writing, and reading or anything else, which naturally captures our mind's attention. The almost magical thing about Mind Maps is that they help ignite interest in any subject at hand making learning feels effortless.

Mr. Tony Buzan, the inventor of Mind Maps, has helped millions of people across the globe realize and discover the potential of Mind Maps. Mind Maps have an extremely large canvas of application and have been scientifically proven to enhance our thinking ability. Our "thinking" is the fundamental block of creativity, which once stretched using techniques such as Mind Maps never falls back to its original dimensions. Thus Mind Mapping is about thinking creatively. And there is no reason to believe why this creative thinking process cannot be applied to the most important formal discipline for manmade creation i.e. Project Management.

A project needs creativity both in defining the end product or service, and during the course of the journey towards realizing that goal using a variety of project management techniques. This book touches both topics though the focus is more on the journey or how the current set of Project Management techniques can be made even more potent by injecting Mind Maps.

Though globally people are already using Mind Mapping for Projects, this book will help you maximize the opportunities for applying Mind Maps along the complete project cycle right from inception to closure. This is an attempt to synergise the two subjects of Project Management and Mind Maps to create an explosion of creativity, which could leapfrog Project Management methodologies to the next level. This book aims to highlight the immense potential and applications of Mind Maps in Project Management. You would be able to discover yourself how Mind Maps make Project Management more visual, more transparent, more engaging and consequently more profitable.

How to Best Use This Book

"Project" as a term is generally and loosely applied to a range of initiatives across industry. Anything from writing a book to setting up a multibillion dollar plant can and must be classified as a "Project". "Project" and "Project Management", therefore, have an extremely wide canvas of application. Mind Maps also combine enormous flexibility and can be easily applied to innumerable areas and situations in organizations. Bringing together these two versatile and widely used tools – project management and Mind Maps - on a single platform results in exciting opportunities, which allows you to capitalize on best practices and strengths of both.

The underlying intent behind this book is to help identify, present and maximize opportunities to beneficially use Mind Maps along a project lifecycle. Though project lifecycles may hugely differ from each other, they all fundamentally cannot escape a start, middle and an end phase. Irrespective of the genre of your project, you can, therefore, discover ideas and opportunities from the chapters dedicated to these three inseparable phases of the project.

You can draw Mind Maps either by hand or using a computer software. It is a good idea to experiment the first few Mind Maps using a freehand and then moving to computer drawn Mind Maps. A number of Mind Mapping Softwares are easily available and their basic versions are mostly free downloads. I have used iMindMap software to create all the templates in this book. I find that it serves well my purpose for all Mind Mapping activities. The book does not focus on individual technical capabilities of Mind Mapping tools for managing projects but on a more fundamental usage of Mind Maps independent of the software you finally choose to use.

There are about 40 Mind Map templates, specifically for managing projects, with their detailed descriptions included in this book. While some of these are specific to project examples, most of them are of a general nature for use across the board in projects. You could get inspired by these to create your own Mind Maps. The primary advantage of this approach is that it lets you immediately capture the specificity of your projects.

Alternately, you could start by using these templates as they are, which could help you come up to speed with Mind Map application in your projects. With a copy of this book you get free access to all the Project Management Mind Map templates (in the file format usable by iMindMap) which are included in this book. All you need to do is drop me a mail at maneesh.dutt@outlook.com with the subject "Enable Access to PM Mind Map Templates" and I will activate the access for you.

Keep in mind that this is a paradigm shift in the way we approach and manage projects. The key, therefore, is to experiment with an open mind and allow some time for the "neurons" in your brain to get adjusted to this new way of managing projects. And every time you experience success with a Mind Map in your project, I would love to hear from you and also, if possible, include your Mind Map in subsequent editions of this book. On that note, "Happy Mind Mapping"!

Chapter 1

Project Management-Mind Maps: The Perfect Marriage!

"A project is all about creation but managing projects demands creativity"

PROJECT MANAGEMENT: Creativity in Creation?

Project Management is known to have been in existence since the Egyptian era and it evolved over centuries driven by growing project complexities and the desire for "speed" in projects aka "Time-to-market". From the 1950's to the 1960s, the defense establishments in the US including NASA, was the main user of Project Management methodologies. In the 1970s, the large engineering and construction companies used project management principles and tools to manage large budget and schedule driven projects. Then in the 80s there was a surge in manufacturing companies and coming of age of the software development sectors, which began adopting advanced project management practices [5]. It is, however, only in the last two decades that project management as a discipline is being widely applied not only by existing but also emerging industries and organizations. From Not-for-Profit organizations to the entertainment industry, there is wide acceptance of the positive value add of the project management discipline.

There are innumerable publications, which address Project Management both as an art and a science. This is the perfect harmony, which would enable a creative endeavor like a Project to flourish. Even a cursory look, however, at the Project Management models and techniques reveals more shades of logic and reasoning than intuitiveness or creativity, which an artist lends to his canvas. Why is this so? Is it that the fundamental definitions of Project and Project Management do not inspire the Project Management Community to do so?

So let's start by investigating these well accepted definitions.

There are many definitions of Project and Project Management, which invariably revolve around the famous PM constraint triangle of Time, Cost and Quality. The PMBOK [3] has adopted the following definition for a *Project*:

"A Project is a temporary endeavor undertaken to create a unique product or service."

"Temporary" implies both a beginning and an end; hence the time and related constraints. On the other hand, "Unique" implies that the product or service is different in a distinguishing way from other products or services. Additionally, the definition focuses on the end result: the product or service.

A project challenges a Project Manager to be "creative" within the defined constraint system of Time, Cost and Quality. The emphasis in the definition is on "temporary" rather than "to create" and on the end product rather than on the elements in the journey of creation. The journey itself appears to be diluted by using the word "temporary". Finally and very importantly, the definition does not in any way focus on the team or human resources responsible for the "creation".

We can thus see that the above definition has a sound logic and strong left brain (rational, logical, order etc.) flavor. This should not come as a surprise given the fact that a good part of the fundamentals for Project Management were developed in a predominantly male dominated society. Times are changing as we shall see shortly.

It is true that "creativity" may not come naturally to all Project Managers, which may possibly explain the high percentage of projects with cost overruns. In such a scenario, any tool which can inject creativity in a Project Management framework is welcome.

But for this, we first need to have a "creative" and more compelling definition for a *Project*, which at the outset demands greater creativity from the project players.

One such proposed definition is:

"A Project is a creative endeavor to build a product or service engaging all the stakeholders meaningfully thereby exceeding or meeting the expectations of the end customer".

In contrast to the usual left brained definitions of a project, we find elements of right ("creative", "engaging", "meaningfully", "expectations...customer") in effect making the definition more holistic. This fundamental shift in definition of a *Project* stresses three important aspects, which are distinct from the traditional Project definitions. Let's see what these are.

First, while the project manager is consciously building a product or service during a project, he may not be conscious of the fact that every project is in effect a "creative" endeavor. The project manager is beginning with a blank slate and possesses complete freedom like an artist to bring the canvas to life. It cannot be emphasized enough that the Project Manager must always be aware of a project being a "creative endeavor" rather than just an end result.

Next, we look at the traditional PM definitions, which tend to lean towards the famous project constraint triangle of Time, Cost and Quality. Experience tells us that every customer has a varying sensitivity to each of these constraints. Some want the product on Time, others within the Cost, and yet some others do not want Quality to be compromised. It is, therefore, important that we keep the "expectations of the end customer" in direct reference rather than other pre-determined constraints. Again more often than not, the customer is not satisfied just with his expectations being met but usually has an unstated desire for more. The definition, therefore, does not limit itself to "meeting" but also includes "exceeding" customer expectations. This stretch in a *Project* definition is definitely desirable not only from the customer standpoint but at the same time it is more than likely to inspires creativity on the part of the project manager and the team.

Finally and most importantly, the definition focuses on "engaging all the stakeholders", something which almost all traditional definitions have been silent about. Each second the world is getting more connected. Future projects demand a greater degree of complexity and an increased number of stakeholders to manage. If we, therefore, look at every project as an opportunity to foster, support and enhance existing relationships amongst all the stakeholders; we consciously tend to enhance manifold the successful outcome of the project. Including this in the definition implies that, in a project the priority on building relationships is equal if not more to the priority on building the product. It is this focus, which would enhance engagement and hence the resultant productivity and creativity of the project team, leading to a product, which meets and perhaps exceeds the customer requirements.

Continuing in the same vein, it becomes necessary to also revisit the Project Management definition so that there is an alignment between the two definitions. Let's go deeper into this now.

The PMBOK [3] defines Project Management as follows:

"Project Management is the application of knowledge, skills, tools and techniques to project activities to meet the project requirements"

We need to enlarge this definition also as indicated below to be in line with the new definition proposed for a *Project* in the last section:

"Project Management is the engagement of knowledge, skills and experience to a project with an intention to increase manifold the probability of its success."

The key points of difference between the two are as follows:

"Engagement" Vs "Application": Given that projects are executed by people/teams, it is necessary that this gets captured in the definition of Project management. "Engagement" is the glue between the person and his/her creation, and more the engagement the less the task is likely to feel like work, and more like play.

"Experience" Vs "Tools & techniques": Once again the human element gets emphasized here. "Experience" is something unique to every individual. We gain experience over time, which helps us create and/or implement tools, techniques, methodologies, frameworks and models to execute project activities in the best possible way. The application of tools and techniques as such is a direct manifestation of the knowledge, skills & experience of an individual. Hence a need for it not to be referenced explicitly in the definition.

"Increase manifold the probability of its success": Like an astrologer, the project manager in a way, has to predict the future, the difference being that the project manager additionally holds complete accountability for achieving the end results of the project. Experience tells us that there

is always an element of uncertainty about the final success of the project. By accepting and recognizing this in the definition, we highlight the value addition being brought about by Project Management activities by increasing the chances of success of a project, which is indeed the essence of all project management methodologies.

Having proposed these new definitions, it is also important to acknowledge that the definitions indicated in the PMBOK [3] have served a very useful purpose over the years in establishing Project Management as a solid discipline globally. With the changing times, the new definitions proposed above for *Project* and *Project Management* will help to formally and consciously inject the much needed creativity while managing projects.

The traditional models of Project Management largely follow the waterfall model, which is based on the idea of sequential execution of project phases. This Project Management model took birth in the brick and mortar industry where it was not very difficult to visualize the solid structures of the project emerging as time progressed. With Software Engineering, however, becoming mainstream, this model was found lacking to be able to cater to the frequent changes during the project life cycle.

Thus project management frameworks such as Agile have come into existence. Though Agile owes its birth to the Software Industry, it is interesting to note that Agile principles are now influencing even the brick and mortar industries. And it is clear that with Agile methodologies, we are experiencing a definite increase in creativity in project management.

The principles of Agile [6] though known and in use for a long time were eventually formalized in the Manifesto for Agile Software Development (aka, Agile Manifesto) in 2001 by its 17 co-signatories at The Lodge at the Snowbird ski resort in the Wasatch Range of mountains in Utah. The principles valued:

- ✓ Individuals and interactions over processes and tools;
- ✓ Working software over comprehensive documentation;
- ✓ Customer collaboration over contract negotiation;
- ✓ Responding to change over following a plan.

The Manifesto states that while there is value in the items on the right, for Agile methodologies the items on the left are more valued.

Looking more closely at Scrum, a form of Agile Project management, we find that there is a definite shift in practices from traditional project management to redefining project management as:

- ⊙ MORE *engaging* through practices such as daily huddle;
- ⊙ MORE *fun* through introduction of metrics such as "velocity";
- ⊙ MORE *connected* with the customer with regular incremental packets of projects being delivered as against a single final delivery;

⊙ MORE *focused* on relations between the project team members rather than processes;

⊙ MORE *visual* with concepts like "Dashboard".

The key words in the Agile software development manifesto are "*Individuals and Interactions*", "*Working Software*", "*Customer collaboration*" and "*Responding to Change*". All of these indicate that project management is becoming more holistic and at the same time more focused on essentials.

These positive changes in projects are possibly the wonderful effect of the right brain creativity with more and more women workforce joining the Project Management discipline. The Global Gender Gap Index developed in 2006 addresses the need for a consistent and comprehensive measure for gender equality. The 2012 report [7] reveals the trends observed in the data over the past seven years across 111 countries clearly indicating that 88% of the countries have improved their performance to close the gender gap. We should not overlook this important factor of diminishing gender gap as an important enabler for creativity in various industries.

MIND MAPS: Filling the Creative Gap in Managing Projects

Various recent PM frameworks are constantly making Project Management lean in terms of the artifacts requirement and a bit more people than product centric. But are these enough for creativity to bloom? Maybe not. Still somewhere the basic parameter of success of a project rests on Time, within Budget and full of Quality whereas if the focus were to be on nurturing relationships, success is more likely to follow automatically. And when we talk of relationships, it is not just about the association between the team members but also how the team members relate or engage with the project.

No creative product has ever been made without a deep and continuous engagement of the individuals or team with the project cause. We are at our best when we are fully engaged in a subject. We, therefore, only need to have the means to nurture engagement and creativity would follow. And this is the gap, which Mind Maps seek to fill in the world of Project Management.

Mind Mapping is "the tool" for enabling holistic thinking thus leap frogging not only our productivity but also creativity.

In his book *"How to Think Like Leonardo da Vinci"* [8], the creativity expert Michael Gelb unravels the key principles that Leonardo da Vinci followed in his highly creative life, which anyone can apply in today's world to be more creative. Gelb highlights that the note taking styles of many of history's greatest brains – such as Charles Darwin, Michelangelo, Mark Twain and Leonardo da Vinci – feature a branching, organic structure complimented by lots of sketches, creative doodles and keywords. There is a lot of evidence, which clearly indicates that all the genii of the past had a strong propensity for visual thinking and naturally used Mind Maps.

Tony Buzan, the inventor of Mind Maps, has done years of extensive scientific research, which conclusively proves that Mind Maps are extremely effective thinking tools, which come closest to the way our brain operates.

In his book "*How to Mind Map*" Tony Buzan [1] states that since the dawn of civilization, the world has undergone a number of "Revolutions of the Mind" and he captures the Ages of "Mindkind" as follows:

The Agricultural Revolution/Age: This is 10,000 years of relatively slow growth, beginning with the settling down of the nomads and ending with the Industrial Revolution. The primary focus during this period was on agriculture and trade.

The Industrial Revolution: The Industrial Revolution in a mere 200-300 years transformed both the physical and the conceptual world, and again changed the way we thought and lived. The focus of this Revolution was on machines. Though it started with machines primarily meant to substitute physical labor, it ended with inventions such as the computer and paved a way to the Information Age.

The Information Revolution/Age: This Age dramatically accelerated the pace of change with the human race mining an infinite load of information leading to an 'Information Overload' and the consequent realization that something more was required. The short lived Information Age - less than 100 years since inception to its transformation - gave birth to the Knowledge Revolution/Age.

The Knowledge Revolution/Age: In this age, the focus shifted from gathering data to management of data into meaningful and manageable clusters or in other words, the Management of Data, viz. Knowledge Management. Finally at the end of the 20th century and the beginning of the 21st, we entered the *Age of Intelligence* driven by a need to touch the source of our thoughts.

The Age of Intelligence: The *Age of Intelligence*, and the Management of the Manager of Knowledge i.e. the brain, was ushered in by an explosive growth in brain research, a growing global fascination with the brain and its extraordinary capacities, and the increasing appearance of the brain in all forms of media.

Each of the ages has been increasingly short with each one accelerating the change in the way we work, do business, live and think.

Observing how inventions have evolved over the ages, we can see an interesting trend emerge. As shown in the Mind Map Figure 1.1 (to be read in a clockwise direction starting with the top right main branch first), this can be captured by categorizing the ages as follows:

a) *Age of the Hands & Legs:* During the Agricultural Revolution, people were close to Nature and worked primarily with their hands and legs. The real increase in agricultural production came during the period 1500-1800 AD when man started using handheld tools inspired by the weapons he used during hunting. These handheld tools in effect gave him "super" hands to do the job better. Subsequently the Industrial Revolution (1750–1850 AD) focused on machines, which in a way were an extended expression of our hands and legs. All the primal machines focused on motion of some sort. The desire for productivity and the setting up of factories of mass production were a means of mechanized production or creating "super-arms", which could work tirelessly for mass production. The means of transport such as the car

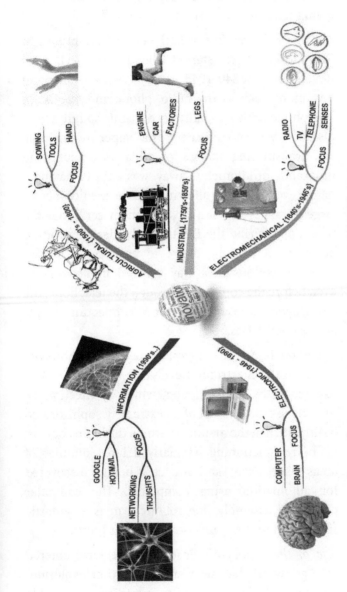

Figure 1.1 Evolution of Innovation over the Ages

and rail engine were an expression of "super-legs" giving shape to our desire for travel and speed.

b) *Age of the Senses:* Towards the end of the Industrial Revolution, there started the Electromechanical Revolution (1840-1946 AD) with emerging inventions such as the radio, phone and television. The phone with its ability to transmit sound across distances was an equivalent of a "super mouth". The TV, transmitting images of what was happening thousands of kilometers away, was akin to having a "super eye". The radio allowing us to hear voices across large distances was similar to a "super ear". Thus the inventions during the Electromechanical Revolution began reflecting our desire to have super senses. These inventions in a way ushered in networking even before the computers through the telephone, the newspaper, radio and television, connecting people across boundaries.

c) *Age of the Brain:* The biggest game changer, however, has been the Electronic Revolution (1946-1990 AD) ushered in by the computer, which in effect was a manmade crude model of an extremely sophisticated brain. Much in the manner in which the brain controls all body functioning, similarly a large number of areas have been, and are still being, discovered for automation using computers. The computer controlled assembly line robotic arm is a fantastic simile akin to the brain controlling our limbs.

d) *Age of the "Thought":* Post 1990, we have entered an Age, which has seen an information explosion. Google with its mission "to organize the world's information and make it universally accessible and useful" has transformed "information" from a source of power to a commodity product. We have also entered into a phase where software has clearly overshadowed hardware to make this world a better place. "Information" and "Software" are like frozen thoughts of individuals in time to be easily reused wherever and whenever necessary. We have, therefore, gone deeper inside the brain, replicating not just what it controls but how it controls. The neurons connect with each other in the brain leading to a new learning. Similarly there are new connections being made on the internet on a daily basis. Unknowingly man has created on the internet a virtual brain thriving on connections.

It thus becomes very clear that over the ages, our creations have been nothing but increasingly a deeper expression of the way our body functions and perceives the world. The ubiquitous software particularly is an equivalent of a "thought" frozen in "space" to be executed in 'time" at human will. We are now trying to understand and manage the fabric of our thoughts by studying the most mysterious object yet discovered in the universe: our BRAIN!

The side effect of the increasingly connected world is an environment, which is best described as "VUCA" i.e. Volatile, Uncertain, Complex and Ambiguous. The notion of VUCA was introduced by the U.S. Army War College to describe the more volatile, uncertain, complex, and ambiguous, multilateral world, which resulted the Cold War onwards [9]. Though the concept existed around the

1990s, it gained in traction subsequent to the 9/11 attack in the US.

Interestingly the human body has a level of complexity and ambiguity, which could have easily given rise to a volatile and uncertain environment but for the BRAIN. In today's world hence we need tools, which mirror the functioning of the brain for not just surviving but thriving in this Age of Intelligence. This is where tools such as Mind Maps come to our rescue, which work on scientific and well researched principles for unlocking our brain's creativity thereby managing the external environment better. Mind Maps have been proven to increase productivity, creativity, recall, enhanced sense of control and fundamentally they help us think better. Learning to use Mind Maps is, therefore, akin to upgrading the Operating System of your brain.

Project Management and Mind Maps: The Perfect Marriage!

A successful project can have different meanings for different stakeholders.

Let's look at the success criteria from the perspective of the three most important stakeholders in a project: the Customer, the Management Team (of the Project Owners) and the Project Team. We could involve even more stakeholders into this framework but all the same this is a good start.

The customer wants a project completed on time, meeting or exceeding the quality requirements for the product or services and within the budget. This is in effect the genesis of the Project Management triangle. As highlighted earlier, an important point to note however, is that the customer may have varying sensitivity to each of these parameters.

The Project's Management would definitely want the project to be within the budget so that they are able to earn the margins they had planned. They would like to have a well-satisfied customer, who is keen to give repeat orders. Finally, success for the management also means that the project team has added experience or skill, which would help their future businesses.

The Project Team's Success lies in meeting or exceeding the customer needs. Additional success factors may include a stronger sense of bonding as a result of the project, enhanced technical/soft skills, new innovations during the project, and finally a sense of achievement of having created something new.

A quick look at the above list of success criteria indicates that there are both right (holistic, quality, team bonding, satisfaction, achievement etc.) and left brain characteristics (on time, budget, margins), which are necessary for the success of projects.

So if the project success criteria include both right & left brain elements, then why should project management tools also not possess similar characteristics? The traditional PM tools from the inception of the discipline of Project Management have displayed a strong left brain bias coupled with an overzealous focus on creating a product or service at any cost. The need of the hour is to induce the creative elements of the right brain to complete the whole picture of success. Once we are convinced about this need in project management methodologies, there will be no better tool than Mind Maps to sharpen and reshape some of the existing PM tools and techniques.

So on one hand, the bride i.e. Mind Maps is full of creativity, is visual, is holistic, organically organized, whereas on the other hand we have the groom i.e. Project Management full of discipline, planning and details in his armor. Is the stage not set for a Perfect Marriage resulting in an explosion of creativity? Is it not time to add to the Holy Grail PM triangle of TIME, COST & QUALITY another MM (Mind Map) triangle, which includes ENGAGEMENT, RELATIONS & CREATIVITY? So how are we going to keep the project team ENGAGED, how will RELATIONS improve as a result of the project and what can be done to really make the project a CREATIVE endeavor?

A lot of project managers around the world are already injecting Mind Maps into their Project management techniques. This book is a humble attempt to formalize Mind Mapping along the project cycle, which may ultimately lay the foundation for a new subject: "Project Management: the Mind Mapping way".

CHAPTER 2

Frameworks for Project Management and Mind Mapping

"You don't have to be a genius or a visionary or even a college graduate to be successful. You just need a framework and a dream" – Michael Dell

Frameworks are like packages of best practices tried, tested and improved over time. Many a times though it would come as no surprise that two organizations follow similar framework of practices but experience very different end results and organizational cultures. In other words what this suggests is that a framework by itself is not sufficient but needs to be complemented by the creativity and discipline of an organization. Creativity is necessary to customize the practices to the organizational business needs, which ensures that the company's standard operating procedures (inspired by the frameworks) support the business end goals. The discipline and consistency with which an organization commits itself to the framework energizes its employees across the hierarchy. Only then can the organization breathe life into the framework and sustain continuous improvements.

Frameworks when used correctly and creatively can play an important role in contributing to the overall efficiency of an organization.

Formal Project Management practices have been in existence for many decades now which is why there are a number of standards and frameworks in existence for Project Management. We look at two Project Management frameworks, which are well accepted around the globe: the PMBOK [3] and the Agile Methodology [6].

For Mind Maps we look at the laws of Mind Mapping as prescribed by Tony Buzan, the inventor of Mind Maps.

Project Management Body of Knowledge

In October 1998, the Project Management Institute (PMI) was accredited as a standard developer by the American National Standards Institute (ANSI).

The PMBOK guide published by PMI is a standard or a framework that describes the nature of project management processes and their purposes. As per PMBOK, Project management processes are grouped into five logical categories:

The Initiating Process Group: comprises all the processes performed to define a new project.

The Planning Process Group: includes processes required to set up the project scope, refine goals and define the course of action to meet the project end objectives.

Executing Process Group: are the processes performed to complete the work defined in the plan.

Monitoring & Controlling Process Group: includes processes required for tracking, reviewing, and regulating project progress and performance.

Closing Process Group: includes the processes performed to finalize all activities to formally close the project/phase.

As per the PMBOK, these five Project Management Process Group consist of 47 project management processes, which are further grouped into ten separate knowledge areas. Each of these knowledge areas represents a complete set of concepts, terms and activities that make up a professional field, project management field or area of specialization. Let's take a simple project example: you need to build your own house beginning with a barren piece of land. In this context, let's detail what the various knowledge areas stand for:

Scope Management: For you, the project scope would be very clear, which is constructing your house on your plot of land. But you need multiple vendors (an architect, mason, carpenter, electrician etc.) and each one of them should know what is expected of them. The onus, therefore, of defining the scope and the boundaries of your expectations of them rests solely on you.

Time Management: You would like to be sure that your new house is ready before the end of the year. For this, you need to define all the necessary activities and timebox them. In the process you would also need to identify resources for each task and the relationship between the tasks i.e. defining what comes when, in a logical sequence moving towards your project completion. Time management, therefore, is about having visibility about the schedule and meeting deadlines. What is important to understand is that time management is still just one aspect of Project Management. Many a times it is mistaken to be the only aspect in managing projects.

Cost Management: This is the easiest to understand. You have to decide on a budget of a million dollars for your house and anything more than this would mean you are exceeding your budget. In the middle of your house construction, the architect suggests that you could have an extra room for a mini-theatre in your plan. You are excited about the idea. You, however, would need to do a cost analysis before jumping to say a yes.

Quality Management: Let's say, you want copper wires of a certain grade and teak wood of a specific brand for your house. These are your quality requirements, which need to be managed through regular quality controls to ensure that you end up with the right product in line with your expectations and minimum defects.

Human Resources Management: Behind every successful project is a motivated team and a creative project manager. The project team is the primary enabler for "creation" in project. Your architect, carpenter, mason, plumber may bring very different personalities to the table. But you as the project manager needs to work on their strengths, manage their weaknesses - and occasional conflicts - to finally have the house of your dreams.

Communications Management: Your architect's reference point for communication could be the drawings that he gets approved from you but your plumber may simply be listening to your oral instructions and making complete sense of it. It is necessary to have a communication plan, which captures all the communications aspects in relation to the stakeholders. A good communication plan goes a long way towards enabling a successful project.

Risk Management: Your planning skills might be good but you may still meet situations, which impact your project progress. A sudden change in weather, labour force going on leave, a stop construction notice from a legal authority etc. are all possible events. Anticipating and quantifying these risks would help plan mitigation actions in advance.

Procurement Management: You need to manage your purchases and this is where procurement management comes to the rescue. For your house construction you "procure" the services of an architect and an interior designer. And additionally, you need all the necessary construction material for your house. Procurement management covers topics, which help plan, conduct, control and close procurements.

Stakeholder Management: As the most important stakeholder, your primary expectation would be to get a house in line with the drawing plans. Your plumber's expectation is to make his margin on the service that he provides, and at the same to keep you satisfied so that you give him repeat and reference business. The most important part of a project manager's job is being aware of each stakeholder's expectations and managing them correctly.

Integration Management: You need to integrate or stitch everything together to create a project plan for use on a daily basis to ensure that the house construction is on track. These day-to-day tasks, which make sure that the project is on track are part of integration management.

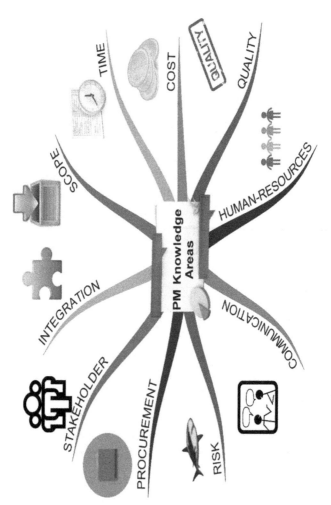

Figure 2.1 *Project Management Knowledge Areas (as per PM BOK)*

The Mind Map in Figure 2.1 captures all these areas. This Mind Map can be developed further in different ways to help the project management process. As an example, the project manager could identify a person responsible, in respective sub-branches of the mind map, for each of these knowledge areas so that all of them are addressed while managing the project life-cycle. Sub-branches to the main branch could also be used for capturing one or two most important deliverables/document You need to manage your purchases and this is where procurement management comes to the rescue for the respective knowledge area. This would give visibility on how the respective areas are getting formalized in the project. This is an introductory Mind Map template and we will review in detail more templates after understanding the laws of Mind Mapping.

There are best practices in the above knowledge areas elaborated in the PMBOK [3]. These require customization from project to project though the basic principles stay the same.

Agile Methodology

Agile truly belongs to the new and emerging trends in Project Management with a focus on iterative and incremental product development, and most importantly, lean governance. Iterative and incremental product development ensure that there are multiple and continuous touchpoints between the project team and the customer. On the other hand, lean governance gives a sense of empowerment and responsibility to the project team to self-correct itself as and when necessary.

While Agile is a framework or a set of principles, there have been number of practices, which have evolved around these principles. The popular Agile methodologies include [6] Scrum, Extreme Programming (XP), Kanban, Agile Unified Process (AUP) and Dynamic Systems Development Method (DSDM).

The Agile practice, which has gained good traction around the globe in a variety of industries, is Scrum. The Scrum method has three distinctive aspects, which give it an individuality, quite different from the usual project management practices.

First, there is no Project Manager's role in Scrum. Instead of having a Project Manager as the nodal point of reference, the project responsibilities are distributed over the three roles across the Scrum Team, namely, the Product Owner, who manages the *product* (and ROI), the Scrum Master for managing the *process* and the team managing *itself* or is self-organizing.

Second, the development happens in time boxed cycles of work called Sprints. Each Sprint is no more than one month each and Sprints take place one after the other without a pause. At the beginning of each Sprint, a cross-functional team selects items (customer requirements) from a prioritized list. The team commits to complete the items by the end of the Sprint. The Sprints are time boxed i.e. they end on a specific date whether the work is completed or not, and are never extended.

Third, given the short development cycles within the sprints, there is a need to have focus on inspection and adaptions. The daily Scrum meeting, conducted as a stand-up meeting, addresses this aspect of "inspect and adapt". The team meets to communicate and synchronize its work. This meeting is for the team to continuously assess its own progress towards achieving its Sprint goal and NOT for reporting progress to the Scrum Master or Product Owner or anyone else. A very important part of the Daily Scrum is the visual management of the tasks on a Project Dashboard-- visible and accessible to all.

There are added nuances in Scrum. The three listed earlier capture well the spirit of Scrum in practice.

The Scrum framework helps in defining the deliverable in smaller segments. At the same time, it allows deep customer involvement for continuous improvement as the project unfolds. Finally, it enables self-management of the teams along with offering opportunities to the team to celebrate at the end of every Sprint.

Given the positives of Scrum, it is no surprise that it is being accepted very well across the globe. Moreover, with the focus on visual and transparent Project Management in Scrum, there is an ample opportunity to use Mind Maps and make this approach to manage projects even more powerful.

Getting started with Mind Maps

"The human brain does not think in toolbars and menu lists; it thinks organically like all natural forms, like the human body's circulatory and nervous system, or branches of a tree and veins in a leaf. That's how the brain thinks. To think well it needs the tool that reflects that natural organic flow. The Mind Map is that tool." - Tony Buzan [10]

A Mind Map is a very simple thinking tool, which helps to crystallize our thought process on paper. We start with the topic to Mind Map in the center of the paper then radiate out sub-topics or ideas in all directions as the rays of the sun. Equipping the current and future generation with this new age teaching, learning and thinking tool holds great potential to unlock one's creativity in one's chosen field.

On the face of it, Mind Maps may look deceptively simple to the point of undermining their immense potential. The extensive research by Mr. Tony Buzan, inventor of Mind Maps, has revealed 7 steps to be followed for making effective Mind Maps [1]:

1. Start in the CENTRE of a blank page in a landscape layout and not portrait layout, which we ever so often use. This allows the brain the freedom to spread out in all directions and to express itself more freely and naturally.

2. Use an IMAGE or PICTURE appropriate to the central idea. This helps to enhance imagination and focus.

3. Use COLORS throughout. Colors add extra vibrancy and life to our Mind Map, imparting tremendous energy to our Creative Thinking.

4. CONNECT your MAIN BRANCHES to the central image. As our brain works by association, hence connect the second and third level branches to the first and second levels, etc., enabling better understanding and recall.

5. Use CURVED branches rather than straight-lined because straight lines are boring for our Brain.

6. Use ONE KEY WORD PER LINE to allow the Mind Map greater power and flexibility.

7. Use IMAGES throughout remembering the old adage that an image is worth a thousand words.

For those new to Mind Mapping, keep in mind that in this book there are two types of Mind Maps drawn; one which need to be read in a clockwise fashion starting from the topmost branch on the right side of the Mind Map and others in which the sequence is not important. Based on the subject being addressed by the Mind Map it would be easy for you to discern this and interpret accordingly.

The above seven steps, sometimes also referred to as the seven laws of Mind Mapping, are in effect the framework for making impactful Mind Maps. These laws are captured in the Mind Map in Figure 2.2 (reproduced from *"The Mind Map Book"* [11]). Once we start using these rules while creating our Mind Maps, the process becomes even more engaging utilizing the complete cortical skills of our brain. All artificial creations we see around had "thought" as the most basic building block. Thus if we can somehow improve the "thought" process, we would have a whole new building block and a whole new creation around it. Behind every manmade creation is a project and behind every project are formal or informal Project Management methodologies that enable their creation.

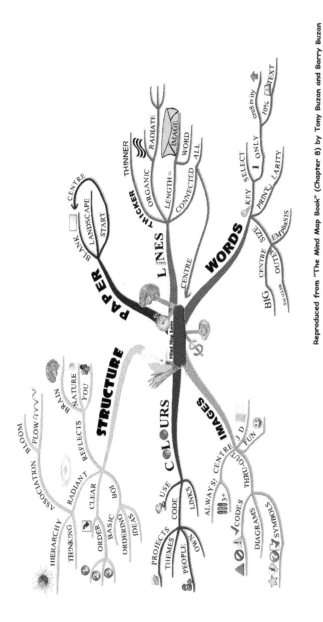

Figure 2.2 Laws of Mind Mapping

Having understood the frameworks for Project Management and Mind Map, we are ready to begin our exciting journey to unravel how Mind Maps can bring in a breath of fresh air to enrich and help graduate from the existing practices of Project Management taking them to the next level. Over a period of time, this should well result in a paradigm shift in the way we manage projects. Though Mind Maps have a much wider canvas of application, they hold the potential to impact Project Management methodologies in a way similar to what Windows operating system did to the world when it replaced DOS. The Windows Operating System added color, images (icons) and flexibility - the existing principles of Mind Mapping - and which also led to the runaway success of Windows.

It is time to upgrade the operating system of Project Management to cater to the new age and generation using Mind Mapping.

Chapter 3

The Subtle "Nature" in Project Management and Mind Maps

"Man strives with reasons while nature thrives on seasons"

There is much to learn from nature all around us. There is an intelligence, which exists in Nature, a little subtle for human intelligence but definitely discernible, though not always understood. Nature has a visible side, which is immediately seen and appreciated by our senses. There are, however, also not so visible forces, which precede creation in Nature. To explain more plainly, while we can "sense" a tree as a creation in Nature, it is not so easily apparent how a small seed with an empty space deep inside transformed itself into a huge tree. Similarly, we can "sense" the universe and our reasoning can take us to the point of birth of the universe. But to fathom that the entire universe was present in an infinitely small speck at the time of Big Bang goes beyond reason and intelligence. But in spite of this mysterious side, we can still pick some precious gems from Nature and grow with the seasons beyond the shores of reasons!

Let's look a little closely at Project Management and Mind Mapping to discover the "natural" laws hidden within them.

PROJECT: *A story from the cradle to the grave*

A project is a process, which leads to an external visible creation starting from internal invisible nebulous ideas and thoughts.

A project cycle has three distinct phases and it is not too difficult to intuitively understand that the human life cycle and the project life cycle have some common threads. Let's take a quick look at the three broad phases in any project [12]:

Birth, a tentative start: We start our life discovering and learning new things everyday as children. As children our energy levels are extremely high but productivity in terms of contribution to the society would be minimal. Similarly at the time of project start, the "newness" of everything gives a high to the team energies. The project is still taking shape and is definitely not contributing to the sponsor's bottom line at this time but holds the promise of a future success. In the same way, a child is nurtured for a potentially fulfilling life in the future. The focus is on creating a safe and healthy environment for the child.

Though project ideas need nurturing like a child, there is an important point of difference -- the ultimate aim is the successful commercialization (or implementation) of the project. The need hence for a project feasibility analysis before resources are committed to the project. In a similar vein, just as a tree may produce hundreds of seeds but only a percentage of these result in a tree so not all project ideas mature into full-fledged projects. Nature has its checks and balances so that only the strongest of the seeds are able to survive and grow. In the same manner, our feasibility check at the start of the project should be strong and robust enough to allow for only the best of the ideas to thrive. Once the feasibility has been successful, resources are assembled to take the idea to its conclusion.

Middle Age, The Productive years: Seeds and children both need an environment to grow. The resources we put together for a project help create an "environment" for transforming the idea into reality.

We move from childhood to adulthood and middle age, which corresponds to our most productive years. There is a certain momentum that we gain in our life since we have a better clarity of where we may want to reach. During this phase, we experience our most important milestones such as marriage, children, material success etc. and also take head on some of the big challenges of our life. We manage risks, relationship issues, material losses and at times loss of our loved ones.

Similarly, in projects, this is the phase when resources consumption is at its peak-- the team is most productive and is in the thick of the execution. Though execution involves reaching the project milestones, it is not without challenges and opportunities along the way. Again the project manager and team need to manage risks, relations, resolve conflicts and face situations where a "loved one" or a team member may decide to part ways midway into the project.

Finally an important point, the earlier an error is discovered and corrected along the project life-cycle, the lower will be the cost of correction. Similarly in our human lifecycle, maximizing our mistakes early on in life is not as harmful as taking bigger risks later in life.

Thus parallels exist in more ways than one between the execution phase and our mid-life.

Old Age, a happy closing: The end phase of a project represents our gradually declining productivity similar to our old age, ultimately culminating in the closure of the chapter of life. In projects too, the rate of consumption of the resources and the output is at its lowest during this phase. The team has completed the project lifecycle and moved into a phase of "reflection" before disbanding and starting a new project. Like the great boxer Muhammad Ali said "Old age is just a record of one's whole life", similarly at this point in project the records are archived and lessons learnt noted for use in future projects. At the end of a lifetime, we are a very different person from what we were when the journey started; similarly by the time we complete a project, we are not the same as we were at the time of start of the project. Events and learnings along the project keep on impacting us and no project fails to transform something in us, however small it may be.

Looking at these parallels between Project management and Nature or life, we realize that there is room for applying principles from Nature to project management and vice versa.

In summary the focus of Project Management is to enhance the probability of achieving an "external" visible creation beginning with "internal" thoughts and ideas. The success, therefore, of the creation being attempted through a project, is dependent on our thinking process and this is where Mind Maps can help.

MIND MAPS: *The "natural" thinking tool.*

Our thoughts are a precursor to every creation or, in context of a project, its final deliverable. But how do we make sure that we are using the complete potential of our brain when thinking, especially while thinking about new ideas and facing challenging situations in projects? We will now see how Mind Maps are aligned to the internal structures in our body and to creation in the external natural world. This makes a Mind Map the perfect bridge to connect our thoughts to an intended creation or outcome. Let's see how Mind Maps are so close to nature.

Nature is Radiant: When we look closely, there is a radiant pattern in every creation of nature whether a flower, snowflakes, trees etc. In fact if we go back in time by 14 billion years (the estimated age of the universe) to the Big Bang, we would find that creation began from a singular point from which the recipe material for the formation of the universe spewed in all directions or radiated in all directions from a center point. Thus going by the popularly accepted theory the original creation was a "radiant" act. And so is our thinking. The moment we hold a thought within our brain, we start getting additional thoughts radiating out from this central thought. Thus our every thought is like a mini Big Bang in our head and the strongest of those get transformed into creation by our hands. In a Mind Map, information is structured in a way that mirrors exactly how the brain functions - in a radiant rather than a linear manner. A Mind Map literally 'maps' our thoughts, using associations, connections and triggers to stimulate further ideas. Thus a Mind Map supports the natural internal system of our brain and the external nature.

Nature is connected: Observe a tree and you will find that every leaf of a tree is connected to every other leaf on the tree through the network of its branches, trunk and roots! Similarly a river emerging from a glacier may eventually form separate tributaries but we can still see the connections between all the tributaries and the mother river in satellite images. Nature thrives on connections. In fact, Leonardo Da Vinci captured this essence very well when he said that "Everything connects to everything else" many years before science even began thinking in that direction. Going deeper inside our anatomy we find similarities to the tree. Every cell in our body connects to every other cell. It is no surprise then what research shows: the brain likes to work by association and connect every idea, memory or piece of information to other ideas and concepts [13]. A Mind Map also thrives on connections, some of which become immediately visible to us but there are other connections which we discover as our Mind Map evolves with every new word, image and idea posted on it.

Nature does not manifest itself in straight lines: The easiest way to tell if something is manmade or nature-made is to check if it has straight lines (unless it is a 3-D copy of something natural like a wax apple)! Taking a walk in Nature, you can discover yourself that you do not see any straight lines whereas sitting in a manmade room, you will probably lose count of the number of objects with straight lines, beginning with the shape of the room itself. Even when we look at the human body, we find a number of gentle curved lines and not straight lines; a robot, however, is full of sharp lines in its anatomy. Robots though may slowly become better copies of the wonderful human body! There are no straight lines in Nature. Neither does the brain like straight lines. It is in line with this that Tony Buzan [1] advocates the usage of curved and not straight lines in a Mind Map to keep the brain better engaged. The brain gets attracted to patterns, which are a combination of randomness and order, just what a Mind Map has to offer.

Additionally, the overall Mind Mapping process involves a unique combination of imagery, color and visual-spatial arrangement, which has been proven to significantly improve recall when compared to conventional methods of note-taking and learning by rote [13]. The brain loves color, images and association. That is exactly the reason why a movie remains etched in our memory for a longer time in comparison to the written word. Mind Mapping brings together our left brain (words, logic, numbers etc.) and right brain skills (curves, color, rhythm, images etc.) making our brain's performance more synergistic. This means that each cortical skill enhances the performance of other areas so that the brain is working at its optimum.

Thus we find that there is a subtle Nature existing in both projects as well as Mind Maps. The project lifecycle is a mini human lifecycle resulting in a product or service.

On the other hand, Mind Maps have well embodied both the principles of creation in nature and the creativity of nature.

Project lifecycle descriptions vary from being very general to being extremely detailed depending on the project type and industry for which the project is being executed. Irrespective, however, of these varying project lifecycles from industry to industry, we find there is real inspiration drawn by both Projects and Mind Maps from Nature and its creations. Bringing both these subjects together in the right admix would help us improve both our internal environment (i.e. our thinking) and the consequent external environment (i.e. the creation from our projects).

In the chapters that follow, we will first take a look at some key general management skills which are essential throughout the project life cycle of the project. We will further discover multiple opportunities how Mind Maps can help us enhance project success by strengthening our project management skills. In subsequent chapters, we focus on the Mind Mapping opportunities along the project lifecycle by phases of the project from birth to execution, and finally the closure of the project.

CHAPTER 4

Key Project Management Skills and How Mind Maps can Magnify them

"A Project Manager is an astrologer with an added responsibility to meet each & every prediction of his."

Along the three phases of a project - start, execution and closing - there are certain key "must-have" management skills necessary for any Project Manager to steer a project correctly from inception to completion. In this chapter, we focus on these key management skills and how Mind Maps can help us further strengthen them.

The project management discipline involves planning, organizing, directing and controlling the company resources towards successful completion of a project without compromising on customer satisfaction. To this end, the Project Manager is given authority (in line with the company guidelines) over a set of company resources; both material and human. The Project Manager is in effect like a mini-CEO accountable for the final outcome of the project. The PMBOK [3] highlights the following five key general management skills that are highly likely to affect most projects:

(i) Leading

(ii) Communicating

(iii) Negotiating

(iv) Problem Solving

(v) Influencing the Organization

In addition to the above, there are three other key skills that are extremely important for project and team success, which are:

(vi) An attitude of learning and improvement

(vii) A Sense of Urgency

(viii) Ability to embrace ambiguity

Let's look at how Mind Mapping can help to enhance each of these skills further:

(i) Leading

Leading is the ability to give a compelling vision accompanied with "execution" pointers for reaching it. The project manager needs to motivate and magnetize his team towards the vision or the end goal of the project.

"Vision" is all about "visualizing" and hence intrinsically related to our faculty of "seeing", helping us capture images all around. The project vision enables us to see a creation in the future using images currently available in the brain's repository. Images are the "high speed" language of the brain compared to words. The Mind Map fundamentally being an image is a very effective vehicle to communicate a project vision, and more so, a collaborative image for the complete team.

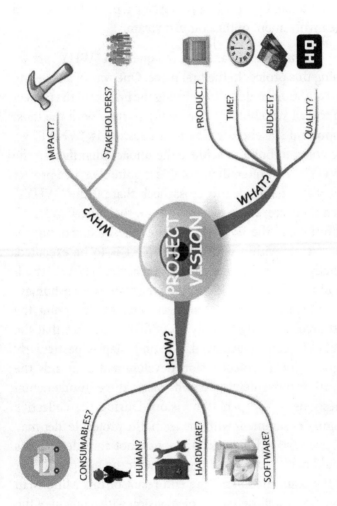

Figure 4.1 Mind Map template for developing a Project Vision

Any good Project vision has to start with a strategic "WHY" before answering more tactical questions on the "HOW" and "WHAT". The simple Mind Map template illustrated in figure 4.1 helps develop a project vision with the involvement of the complete team.

The first branch answers the question "WHY" are we doing this project in the first place. One way of answering this question could be identifying the impact of the project on the all stakeholders, preferably starting with the most important stakeholder. The next question is "WHAT" we are going to build to achieve the impact identified in the "WHY". More often than not this is quite clear in a project but it is a good idea to crosscheck that all the "WHYs" identified are answered by one or the other "WHAT". Additionally, the "WHATs" are the time, quality or budget constraints within which this project is to be executed. Finally we come to the third branch, the "HOW" which would in effect mean identifying the resources i.e. human, consumables, hardware, software etc. At this point the resources are only broadly identified to be sure that the "WHAT" can be achieved. A Mind Map is particularly suitable for a project vision development as it aids the iterative movement between these three fundamental questions to "deepen" the vision. During the collective vision development with the team, the project leader may receive several feedbacks previously not considered. This would help to enlarge the vision with the perspectives of all the team members. The end result of this Mind Map would be a well-defined project vision with a buy in of the complete project team. The project manager could do well to circulate this Mind Map along with the Project Vision statement to the stakeholders involved.

(ii) *Communicating*

Communication involves the exchange of information with dimensions beyond being just written or oral. In the context of a Project environment, we can categorize information as External or Internal. The external communication flow is more formal (i.e. reports, briefings, minutes etc.) whereas the internal communication would necessarily have a fair degree of both formal and informal (ad hoc conversations, memos etc.) communication flows. The communication flow within the organization could be vertical (along the hierarchy i.e. with the boss and team) or horizontal (with peers).

Project Communications management includes the processes required to ensure timely and appropriate generation, collection, dissemination, storage and final disposition of project information. A good project communication plan is an important element in building relationship with all the stakeholders. A communication plan is made at the start of the project and ideally presented during the kick off meet itself for approval and feedbacks from the stakeholders. An example of a communication plan in the form of Mind Map is given in Figure 4.2 [12]. This Mind Map helps build a communication plan using the four elements in project: meetings (primarily oral communication forums), reports, escalation and an important but many a times ignored aspect, recognition including the team celebrations.

Meetings: This branch of the communication plan helps list all the oral communication forms possible during the project lifecycle. Broadly, there is an opening or a kick off meet, intermediate review meets and finally a closing

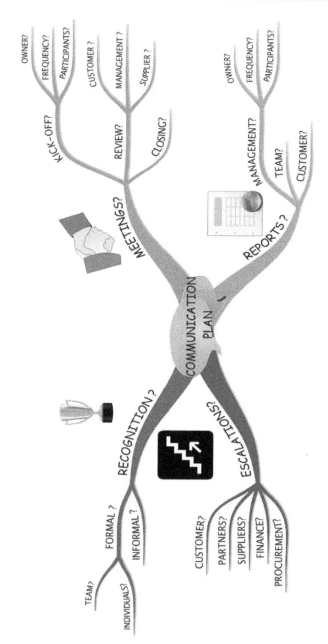

Figure 4.2: *Mind Map template for defining a Project Communication Plan*

meet along a project lifecycle. The review meets in turn could be board review meets primarily for customer or progress review with the management and could also involve reviews with critical suppliers. For each meet, it is important to identify the primary responsible for the meeting conduct, the frequency of the meet and the participants. As an example, for the kick off meet the primary responsibility could be with the project manager and it would be held at the start of the project with the participation of all the stakeholders. Similarly, the other meets are defined and recorded in this Mind Map.

Project presentation is integral to many project meets, especially those involving the multiple stakeholders of the Project. Mind Maps have been found to be an effective medium for first structuring the thoughts of the presenter and then creating a positive impact on the audience. Mento et al. [14] found that executive students using only Mind Map for presentations were able to handle challenging questions with confidence. They had better recall of the information because it was captured and stored in an integrated, radiating manner rather than linearly.

Reports: The reports primarily include the written communication necessary for transparency and information exchange in a simple and quick way. The reports from the project owner's perspective can be either internal or external communication. The internal communication would include reports and minutes for circulation within the project team. Whereas external communication encompasses the formal reports required by stakeholders, such as customer, suppliers, legal bodies etc. Similar to meetings, each of the reports should have an identified owner (or author), frequency of release and listing of participants to whom the reports are circulated.

Escalations: There could be times in a project when a speedy resolution of an issue may call for an escalation beyond the usual hierarchy executing the project. It is imperative that these escalation points are identified for each stakeholder and communicated across to mitigate showstoppers along the project progress. The next Mind Map branch records these escalation points across stakeholders (customer, partners, critical suppliers etc.) as also internal company functions (finance, procurement etc.), if necessary.

Recognitions. In the thick of a project and associated emotions, there is always a danger that team efforts do not get recognized. Project managers would do well to acknowledge "Recognition" as a mandatory step in any project. To ensure that this is not missed out and to keep the team motivated, this element should and must be recorded in any project communication plan. Recognitions could either be formal or informal. Formal recognitions and team celebration points should be communicated transparently on this Mind Map at the start of the project. These include items such as team dinner linked to an important milestone or individual recognition for exemplary work performed etc. Informal and impromptu recognitions such as a thank you note, a pat on the back etc. can be left to the discretion of the project manager to either include or otherwise in the communication plan.

The communication plan is defined at the start of the project and later revised, if needed, with the progress of the project. It is vital that this Mind Map itself should be widely and frequently communicated across the team so that it becomes second nature to everyone.

(iii) Negotiating

As per PMBOK [3] negotiating involves conferring with others to come to terms with them or reach an agreement.

During the course of a project the likely items for negotiation include time, cost or budget, quality requirements and the project scope. Moreover, negotiation could involve either two parties or multiple stakeholders in the project.

The essential aspect of negotiation is to understand the interests of all the stakeholders and the cost they are willing to incur in the event of a solution not being to their expectation. The Mind Map in Figure 4.3 captures landscape of possible Benefits versus Costs (or risk) for alternative solutions being placed on the negotiation table. Once the benefits and costs stand identified vis-à-vis the stakeholders involved (e.g. Customer, Management & Team in this example, it is easy to trace possible strengths and weaknesses in one's proposal. This would help effectively steer the negotiations to a beneficial solution. If necessary, some form of scoring could also be used to quantify the benefits and costs/risks to help determine the most favorable solution. Such a Mind Map if done before hand would immensely help during the actual negotiation meeting.

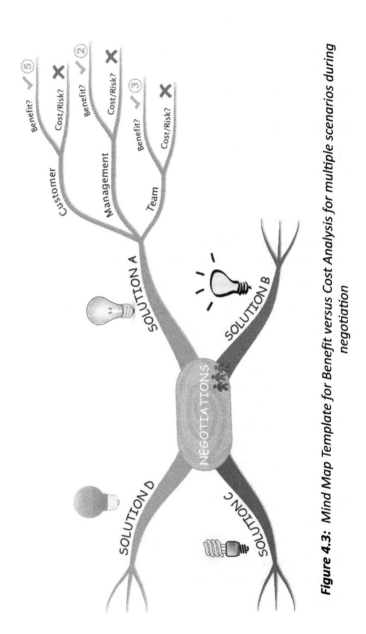

Figure 4.3: *Mind Map Template for Benefit versus Cost Analysis for multiple scenarios during negotiation*

Alternatively, in his book "*Getting to Yes*" [15], Roger Fisher proposes four steps for effective negotiations:

1) Separate the people from the problem

2) Focus on interests, not positions

3) Insist on using objective criteria

4) Invent Options for Mutual Gain

The above method in effect changes the way we visualize negotiations. A typical image of negotiation is seeing two parties on either side of the table slugging it out to win. Whereas with the above steps a new image emerges in which both the parties are sitting on the same side fighting "together" against the problem projected on the wall in front of them.

A simple but powerful Mind Map for negotiation could be made using the above four steps with a branch for each of the steps as indicated in Figure 4.4. The first branch would help identify the core issue or problem independent of the people. The fundamental question to be answered over here is "WHAT" is the core issue independent of the people? The second branch is an important one, which helps unveil the interests of the individual parties. The third branch of the Mind Map identifies the objective criteria for the issue at hand. So in case the project manager needs to negotiate an increase in the project cost, he would need to use some standards to objectively qualify the increase in cost. Such criteria could include manpower or material costing standards. Similarly, there could be other benchmarks or references. The first three branches would give a fair idea of possible solutions, which are then captured on the last branch.

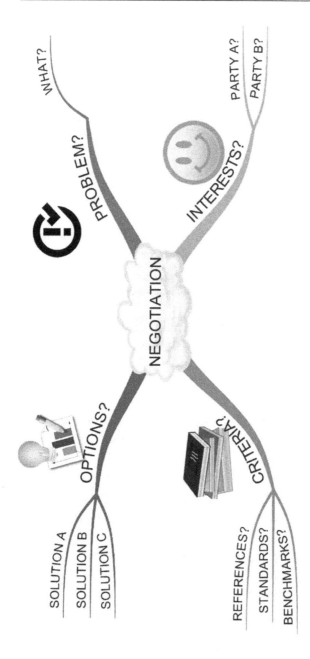

Figure 4.4: *Mind Map template for Negotiation using the principles in "Getting to Yes" by Roger Fisher.*

In case of each solution, the gain and advantages for either party can be identified to facilitate the selection of the best solution. A good way to approach the matter would be that each party makes its own Mind Map, which could be presented in a joint meeting to come out with the final map and a possible outcome to overcome the deadlock.

(iv) Problem Solving

There will always be innumerable opportunities to solve tough problems during the course of any project. The PMBOK [3] refers to problem solving as a combination of problem definition and decision making. Problem definition requires distinguishing between causes and symptoms whereas the decision making involves problem analysis and selecting the most appropriate solution.

A Mind Map can help think with greater clarity to explore relationships between ideas and elements in an argument thereby increasing the probability of generating creative solutions. It brings in a fresh perspective to things allowing us to see all the relevant issues and analyze choices in light of the bigger holistic picture. A simple problem solving Mind Map template is illustrated in figure 4.5.The focus of this Mind Map is first identifying the symptoms or the perceived effects of the problem. This is recorded in the first branch answering the question WHAT. This branch should also be used to record the available facts, assumptions (if any) and finally what you intend achieving, viz the final goal. The second branch probes deeper into the cause asking WHY the problem or the issue exists in the first place. This allows possible

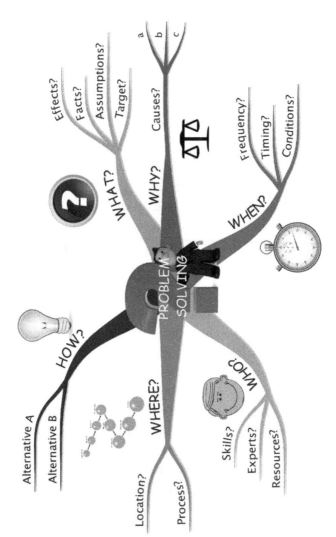

Figure 4.5: *Mind Mapping for Problem Solving using 5 Wife & 1 Husband method.*

causes to be identified within the existing environment. The third branch analyses the timing or the frequency of the problem by answering the question WHEN. What is the number of times the problem has occurred or are there any specific conditions or timings when the problem surfaces. It could also be used to record the timeline by when the problem must be resolved. The next branch attempts to identify experts or possible resources WHO could help in solving the problem at hand. A WHERE branch could also be used to locate the process step or physical location where the problem is observed. It could also represent the environment required for enabling a solution. The last branch attempts possible solutions using the data collected so far by answering the question HOW. Usually the HOW would emerge by solving or mitigating the multiple causes identified in the WHY branch. Once possible alternatives have emerged, they could be further detailed in a separate Mind Map to identify the best possible solution. Chris Griffiths, in his book "*GRASP the Solution*" [2] describes in great detail this method (also known as the 5 Wives and 1 Husband technique) with an emphasis on how it can be used to define a problem completely and minimize the tendency to jumpstart to a solution.

As an application for using Mind Maps for problem solving describe how Mind Maps used to plan patient care at Front Range Community College resulted in enhanced thinking skills including critical thinking, whole-brain thinking and comprehensive thinking [16].

Influencing the Organization

As per the PMBOK [3], influencing the organisation involves the ability to "get things done" by understanding both the formal and informal structures of all units involved: the performing organisation, customer, partners, contractors and other stakeholders. The Project Manager would need to wield his influencing skills at multiple stages in a project. Hence it is important that the Project Manager is aware of and understands the landscape of the stakeholder he is dealing with. Assuming this stakeholder is the customer, the Mind Map in figure 4.6 allows one to analyse all the critical information for the customer, including the formal and the informal organisational structure [12]. The first branch lists the various products for the customer, which would be of interest from the point of view of the project being undertaken for the customer. The second branch helps identify the existing and potential competitors of the customer. The third branch focuses on the financials of the organisation to get a feel of the financial health of the organisation. A quick look at the important suppliers to the customer could additionally provide important information as a project provider to the customer. Possible risks associated with the customer could also aid strategic business and project decisions. Finally, the last two branches map the organisation's management and the project team. Once this landscape is clear it would not be very difficult to locate the strengths, weaknesses and the levers inside the organisation, which would help facilitate decisions at various points in the project. As an example, we may discover while making the Mind Map that a Project Team member is closely associated

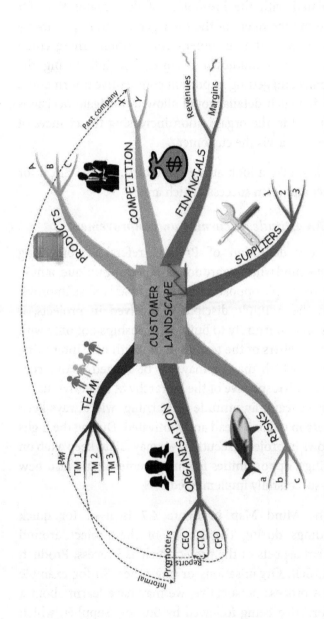

Figure 4.6: The Customer Landscape Mind Map helpful in identifying formal & informal organizational structures and information to influence the organization.

or related with the Promoters of the organisation. Or that some members of the management were previously working with the customer's competition. These could be a hitherto unknown channels for influencing the company and getting important competitive information. Knowing such details would allow to navigate decisions better within the organisation increasing the chances of success vis-a-vis the customer.

Now let's take a look at the three other skills critical for project and team success, which are:

(v) An attitude of learning and improvement

The very definition of Projects refers to something "unique", and when we are doing something unique or new, there are ample opportunities to learn as well as improve. Given the multiple disciplines involved in projects, it offers an opportunity to build relationships not only with other members of the team but also with new interesting subjects, which may or may not be related to our core expertise. Irrespective of the hierarchy of an individual in a project team, an attitude of learning, will always keep the person in good stead and motivated. During the highs and lows in project execution, we may fail to keep a tab on learnings, opportunities for improvements and also new ideas successfully implemented.

The Mind Map in figure 4.7 is used for quick recordings during the course of the project around different aspects of the project such as Process, Product, Team, Self, Organisations or any other. So for example from a process perspective, we may have learnt about a best practice being followed by our key supplier, which

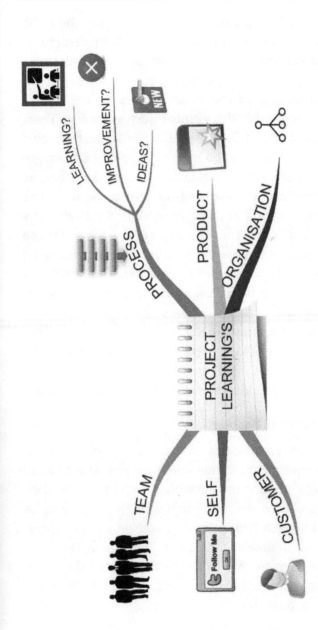

Figure 4.7: *Mind Map template for capturing Learnings, Opportunities for Improvement and New Ideas during the course of the project*

can be easily replicated inside our organisation. An opportunity for improvement could be reduction in the current cycle time for new supplier registration. Finally, a new idea implemented may be a new process for procurement of low value supplies for the project. Likewise across the other elements such as Product, Team, Self, Customer and Organisation, a similar analysis could be undertaken. Each team member should be encouraged to keep a tab on these elements during the course of the project and at the end of the project the respective team member/project manager should collectively share these Mind Maps. The learnings are the value addition for the team; the opportunities for improvement could be prioritized and translated into action; and finally new ideas could then be further shared through publications or protected through various Intellectual Property protection instruments such as patents, copyrights etc. Every project would be replete with such opportunities and the active usage of Mind Map for this purpose would help create a groundswell of all of these for future benefits.

(vi) A Sense of Urgency

In most projects, time is of key essence with a defined end date being a pre-condition for the project definition. If you are working on something without an end date, then be assured you are not working on a project. A sense of urgency hence aligned to the project end goal is very much desirable at all stages. The famous Urgency–Importance matrix by Stephen Covey [17] translated into the form of a Mind Map as given in figure 4.8 becomes even more powerful.

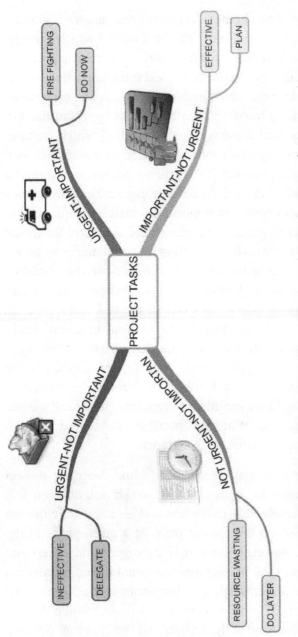

Figure 4.8: *Mind Map template for Time Management based on Steven Covey's Urgency- Importance matrix*

The first branch captures the urgent-important activities. These are the activities, which require immediate attention and include crises, pressing problems or deadline driven projects. Next is the important but not urgent branch, which includes activities like prevention, relationship building, identifying new opportunities, etc. The keyword for this branch is "Plan", which captures activities important for our mission or values and need systematic planning. The challenge would be to complete these tasks before these become urgent. The third branch is the not urgent-not important, which is the quadrant of activities required to be minimized and includes typical time-wasters such as browsing on social media without a specific purpose or watching something on the television, which do not add on to our learning in line with our goals, some mails, phone calls etc. In the real world context, it may not be possible always to drop these completely. It is hence important to realize that we have the ability to do these later: the punch word for this branch is "do later". The last branch covers the Urgent-Not Important activities. These include interruptions, phone call, certain meetings etc. Wherever possible, we should try and "delegate" activities on this branch.

The best way to use this Mind Map for project planning is to capture all the weekly activities on this map. Usually only important and essential activities are scheduled on the project plan. At a given phase of the project, however, some may be urgent and others not so urgent. The project manager would need to take out time for both though spending more on the "Important" activities. "Urgent" in context of a project would depend on the deadline of the activity and the quantum of work.

It may be difficult to avoid "not important" activities in a project, but being aware about the same could be the first step towards minimizing your time in this quadrant.

Maneesh Dutt et al. in their publication *"The Project Managers Styles"* [18] capture an interesting co-relation between the outward behaviour of a Project Manager at various stages of a project depending on his propensity or leaning towards a particular quadrant. Thus the manager who spends most of the time in the Not Urgent-Important quadrant is the effective Project Manager; the Urgent – Important manager is the Fire fighter; the not-important-urgent is the ineffective manager; and the not urgent-not important is the resource waster.

This Mind Map can also be used as a diagnostic tool to analyse where one is actually spending daily time and then locate the resource wasters. And the path to success in any project would be to focus on all the important activities and doing them with a sense of urgency before they become urgent.

(vii) *Ability to embrace ambiguity*

Given that a Project is a constraint system involving Time, Quality and Cost, there will be occasions where decisions need to be taken with missing or incomplete data points. The later such a situation occurs along the project lifecycle, the greater is the impact of a wrong decision. Many a times, the way out would be a trade-off between Time, Quality or cost. In such scenario, project managers need to take strategic decisions taking into consideration the facts, assumptions and the impact of a given decision.

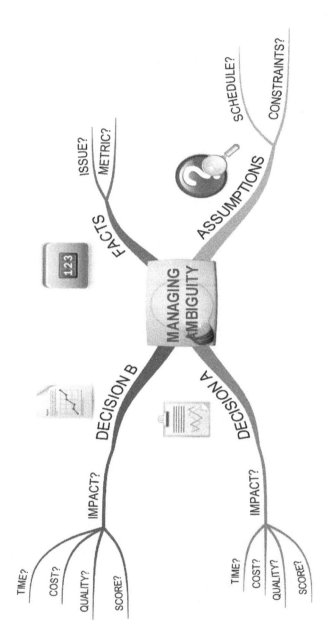

Figure 4.9: *Managing Ambiguity Using Mind Maps*

A Mind Map such as the one in figure 4.9 helps lay down everything on the table thus facilitating the best decision in a given context. The first branch focuses on the facts at hand thereby purely stating the known elements in a situation. This could be capturing things like resources available, impacted metrics for the project such as schedule or cost delinquency, the specific threat (related to the issue) that has arisen like a delayed critical hardware for the success of the project. The second branch helps list the assumptions at a given time. As an example, an assumption could be that a specific hardware for the project could take 3 weeks for delivery or that the customer will not accept any price increase in the project or a delay in the project.

Additionally, at this point it is necessary that you revisit all the facts stated in the previous branch to check if any assumption has been mistaken for a fact. As an example, the criticality of the delayed hardware may be recorded as a fact but while jotting down the assumptions it may be a good idea to question whether the hardware is really critical at that particular stage of the project or not? Once each of the assumptions have been carefully jotted down after careful scrutiny, the next step would be to do an impact analysis of the possible decisions or alternative solutions. For each possible decision, the corresponding negative impact on time, cost or quality is quantified on a scale of 1 (least) to 10 (maximum). If the customer has a greater sensitivity to one of the parameters, it may be useful to give an additional weightage to that parameter. Once done, add the score of the impact for each solution to see which alternative gives the minimum impact and thus the possible preferred solution to investigate further.

This could help provide a well analysed and informed direction to take, arresting the ambiguity, which would have been prevalent prior to this analysis.

In summary, it should be quite clear that Mind Maps can be applied with ease to strengthen further some of the important attributes or management skills required during the course of a project. The project management process varies from one organisation to another but the aforestated management skills are independent of the project being executed. Irrespective of the industry, an organisation can hence still enhance these vital management skills by using Mind Maps for managing projects.

In the next chapter, we go deeper into project phases and discover more opportunities for Mind Mapping along the complete project life cycle enabling individual, and hence organisational, creativity.

CHAPTER 5

The Birth: Initiation or Project Start

"All things are created twice; first mentally; then physically. The key to creativity is to begin with the end in mind, with a vision and a blue print of the desired result." — Stephen Covey

The project start is similar to the arrival of a new born baby in the family. The project idea is new, creates excitement, is full of potential but at the same time fragile and needs protection. The new-born baby will have minimal "resources" demands (as compared to an adult) but a high level of hygiene and safety is a must for the baby's well-being. Similarly, in a project though the effort invested in terms of resources is minimal but the overriding need is to ensure "pure" or "right" resources for the project initiation, beginning with the feasibility. A solid foundation at the time of project initiation would immensely enhance the probability of the project success.

A new baby born in the family implies a new relationship emerging both between the child and the rest of the family; but also it reinforces some existing relationships, the most obvious being the one between the child's parent. In the same way, a new project start should also be seen as an opportunity for developing new relations and strengthening existing relations with the stakeholders. This includes not only the relationship with the external entities (customer, legal bodies etc.) but also among the project team members. A host of issues would be taken care of easily if the project team visualizes the project as a vehicle for enriching relationships through a positive contribution to all the stakeholders involved as there is something for everybody in a Project.

The Initiation of a project comprises the following important aspects:

a) Feasibility: Understanding at a macro level whether the project is actually possible or not;

b) Project benefit analysis: Mapping the quantitative and qualitative benefits for all the stakeholders;

c) Project Charter: The formal internal go-ahead for an organization or team to start the project;

d) Collecting & Prioritizing requirements: Understanding what to build first;

e) Scope Definition: Defining what needs to be built involving the concerned stakeholders;

f) Time Management: Building the "relationship" between the resources and activities with time;

g) Cost Management: Managing the project budget.

h) Skill Assessment: Assessing the skill set of the team member versus needs.

i) Communication: Having an outline of information flow, the what, the when, how and who.

j) Risk & Opportunities Management: Understanding not only the internal and external risks but also the opportunities.

Let's look at each of these aspects individually and discover the opportunities and benefits of Mind Maps therein:

a) FEASIBILITY

The feasibility of the project is a check on whether we would be able to meet the expectations of the customer within the given technical boundaries and the triple constraints of time, cost and quality. The start of feasibility assumes that there is sufficient clarity on the requirements/expectations from the customer and other stakeholders. A good feasibility study ends with adequate clarity and confidence to achieve the project goals, else the management may take a "NO GO" decision till further clarity or the project is finally shelved.

During this phase of the project, the primary focus is to ask as many questions as possible. To assess the strength of the project idea the customer/marketing/design/ development are probed whereas the organizational commitment is assessed by questions to the management.

A number of factors can help decide the feasibility of a project. The Mind Map template given in figure 5.1 helps capture these as follows:

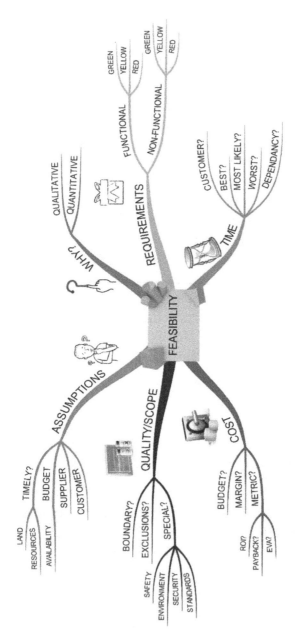

Figure 5.1: *Conducting a Project Feasibility Analysis using Mind Maps*

*Why?:*This is the fundamental question with which the project feasibility starts and hence is the first branch in the feasibility Mind Map. There could be clear quantitative reasons in terms of the expected margins or improved efficiency for the product. But many a times even if the quantitative reasons are not in favor of the project, there could be strategic or qualitative reasons for doing the project. This could include possible future bigger business even if the margins are lower than the threshold benchmark for the organization.

Requirements: At the feasibility stage, the focus is on macro level requirements, both functional and non-functional. Thus the second branch of the Mind Map covers this. Each of the second level branches (functional & non-functional) have sub-branches Green, Yellow and Red for stratification of the requirements. The Green branch captures the easily achievable requirements; the Yellow focuses on the achievable with certain associated difficulty or complexity, and finally the Red, which represents the not achievable or unclear requirements. For the Red items, an additional investigation would be needed to try and shift them to the green or yellow branches. If something still remains in the red, it needs to be checked how it can be removed from the red list, if at all.

A feasibility check with reference to the project triple constraints, of Time, Cost and Quality is a must i.e. is the project achievable within the stated Timeline, the company Budget and the customer's Quality requirements. The next three branches of the Mind Map focus on these three. Before that, however, let us keep in mind that every end customer is unique and would have a varying sensitivity to the triple constraints; some may be very price/cost sensitive, another could be stringent about the delivery quality and still another could be non-compromising about the timelines. This customer perspective or sensitivity can add an important dimension towards enhancing the feasibility study. Let's look at the three constraints:

Time: First, we need to identify the timeline, if any, within which the customer wants the project to be delivered. Next, applying the three point estimation technique we record the *Best case*, *Most likely* and the *Worst case* for the project duration in each of the branch. Finally, should there be any specific dependency on another project that could constrain the delivery date for the current project, then that should also be identified here. With these branches in place, it is easy to check whether the project is possible in the given time frame or not.

Cost: The constraint of cost is many a times the most important one to be adhered to from the project organizations perspective. The important elements such as the budget and the expected margin are captured here. Additionally, any other metric that the organization uses for measuring a project cost performance can also be captured such as ROI (Return on Investment), Payback period, ROS (Return on Sales), Economic Value Add (EVA).

Quality (or Scope): The sub branches of this capture the project boundary and the exclusions. Using a simple example of setting up a factory will make this clear. For the factory project, a certain supplier would be responsible for providing all the engineering equipment in the plant. The exclusions for him, however, may be the utility pipelines. Over and above this, there may be some special needs from the perspective of safety, security, environment or a specific standard. These are captured on a separate sub branch.

Assumptions: The last branch - Assumptions - is perhaps the most important one to delve on carefully since the project assumptions are often overlooked or not formalized. It is important to check the assumptions with respect to the factors identified in the previous main branches. So in effect questions to be asked are such as, are there any hidden or obvious assumptions in the timeline being committed or in the budget being outlaid? What are the important assumptions being taken with respect to the customer and important stakeholders like a critical supplier or a legal agency? Here it is also important to consider generic assumptions not tied to a specific project criteria but say to the micro or macro-economic factors, which could impact the project either negatively or positively.

For projects which are perceived as high risk, there could be additional Mind Maps that can be used to focus better on single aspects such as Risk or Assumptions. An example of Mind Map specifically for capturing assumptions at the feasibility stage is given in figure 5.2. Thomke in his book *"Managing Product and service Development: Text and Cases"* [19] proposes four categories of assumptions for a new idea: Need, Technical, Production and Commercial. The corresponding categories for a new

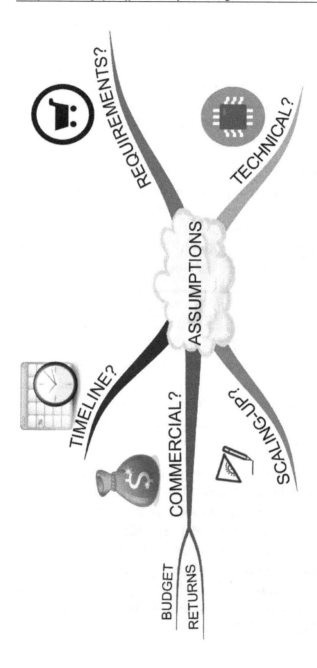

Figure 5.2 *Mind Map template to aid detailing of Assumptions in Projects*

project could be requirements, technical, scaling-up and commercial which are mapped on the individual branches of the Mind Map in figure 5.2. The requirements and technical are self-explanatory. Scaling up or production helps analyze assumptions, if any, to scale up the project from an existing prototype. The commercials would help look at assumptions underlying the budget outlaid for the project and the returns expected. Finally, since a project has to be grounded with a start and an end date, it makes sense to have a separate branch solely to look at assumptions pertaining to the project time line.

All of the above can easily be mapped onto a Mind Map to ultimately check the project feasibility. The sample template of this Mind Map as given in Figure 5.1 can first made by the project manager and then vetted collectively with his management and/or customer to iterate the elements indicated there. Once this feasibility landscape is completed, it would not be difficult to gauge whether to proceed with the project or not, and at the same time it would provide a very good holistic view of the complete project.

Feasibility been checked and assuming a go-ahead to the project we move to the next step of identifying the benefits resulting from the project.

b) PROJECT BENEFIT ANALYSIS

Every project promises to offer a benefit to a major stakeholder (the customer) but are there additional benefits to the other stakeholders, which may be getting overlooked. This is exactly the purpose of Benefit Analysis Mind Map [12] i.e.to check the value add (or even a

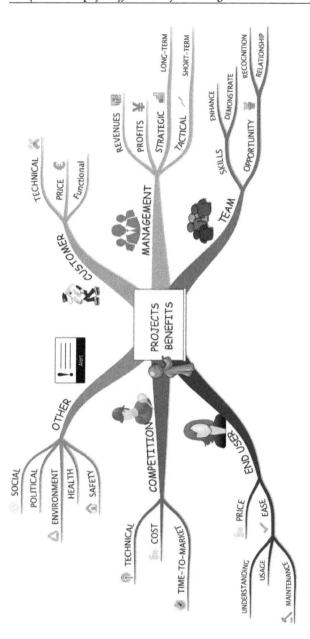

Figure 5.3 *Project Benefit Analysis using Mind Maps*

negative impact) for the stakeholders as a result of the project.

The simple Mind Map in figure 5.3 lists the stakeholders on the main branches starting with the customer. The obvious benefit to the customer could be in terms of the Price, Technical features or some other functional competitive advantage. The project owner could draw quantitative or qualitative benefits from the revenues or profit and/or other strategic or tactical benefits. The next branch focuses on the advantages that the team would gain in terms of the skills enhancement and opportunities for recognition and building new relationship. If the end-user for your final product or service is different from the customer, you could have a separate branch focused on their benefits such as the price and ease of usage etc. You could also include "Competition" as a branch and do a quick check if your project is unknowingly passing an advantage to them. Finally global factors such as Social, Political, Environment, Health, Safety etc. could also be captured in the Map. A powerful use of this Mind Map is to motivate the project team by instilling a stronger sense of purpose once they see the wide impact of their project.

Once the project feasibility analysis has been done and an overview of the benefits identified we move to the next step of building a project charter essential for the formal start of the project.

c)   PROJECT CHARTER

Once the Project Feasibility has resulted in a "GO" decision for the project, the next step is to detail the project charter and the project scope. Though the project charter and scope can be developed in the parallel, it is preferable to first have the project charter. The reason being that the project charter is an internal document for the organization issued by the project initiator or sponsor and once approved can be used as a reference for developing the detailed project scope.

The project charter formally authorizes the existence of a project and provides the project manager the authority to apply organizational resources to project activities [3]. The project charter seeks to define the top level boundaries of the project with sufficient detail to help the organization's management to understand the risks and benefits and thus intelligently sanction the company resources for the project.

A Mind Map very effectively captures the top level view of a subject. For defining a project charter hence where there is a need to put the essential elements of the project together, there cannot be a better tool than Mind Maps. Both from the perspective of using a Mind Map for creating a project charter and from presenting one to the top management, Mind Maps fit the need very well.

The Mind Map in figure 5.4 provides a template for capturing a project charter. This can of course be modulated with the level of detailing required depending on the project complexity. As per PMBOK [3] a Project Charter should encompass the following elements (among others or inter alia) and these are captured on the main branches of the Mind Map in Figure 5.4:

- High level requirements: These are defined on the first branch capturing both the functional

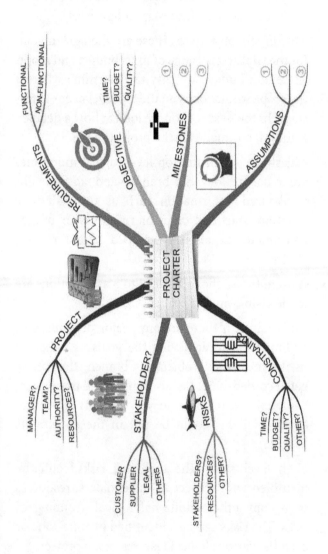

Figure 5.4: *Defining a Project Charter Using Mind Maps*

and non-functional requirements. This branch could be similar to the requirements branch in the project feasibility Mind Map in figure 5.1

- Measurable objectives: These are the agreed goals for the triple constraints of time, budget and scope. Time and budget are easy to determine whereas the scope would focus on the top level needs at this stage. In the next section we look at how a detailed Mind Map is made for the project scope.

- Milestone: Again the top level logical milestones are recorded on this branch, and additionally, if required, information such as the milestone duration, start/end dates or resources or budget consumed can also be mapped here for extra clarity.

- Assumptions: The top level 2 to 3 assumptions are made visible on this branch.

- Constraints: If there are any major dependencies or limitation in achieving the goals as indicated in the measurable objectives branch, then these get recorded here. As an example, if the project completion is to coincide with the start of another event then this could be put in the constraints branch.

- High level risks: The top level risks could be identified with respect to stakeholders, resources or by any other additional logical grouping of risks. The risks can also identified by milestone or even the various logical features of the project.

- Stakeholder identification: This is a detailed listing of all the stakeholders, beginning with the customer to the suppliers and any external legal agencies.

- Project: The final branch focuses on the identification of the project manager, the team, resources and the authority of the project manager.

Many of the elements above are also represented in the project feasibility Mind Map but the nature and purpose of these two Mind Maps are very different. The feasibility Mind Map is more investigative and helps decide whether the project needs to be executed in the first place or not. The project charter, on the other hand, captures the facts and assumptions to enable the management to commit resources to the project.

d) COLLECTING & PRIORITIZING REQUIREMENTS

Once the project charter is clear, the process begins to collect and document the project requirements of the various stakeholders. Given the general complexity of the projects and the technologies at play, it is not uncommon to have situations in projects where the customer does not have full clarity about the priority of their requirements. In such a situation, it becomes important to help the customer classify the requirements in an intelligent way. One very effective model that is in use in the industry is the Kano model [20]. It simply identifies the requirements in terms of their impact on the end customer. Thus the three categories depending on the impact are "Must Have or Basic", "Performance or Linear Factors" and "Excitement factors".

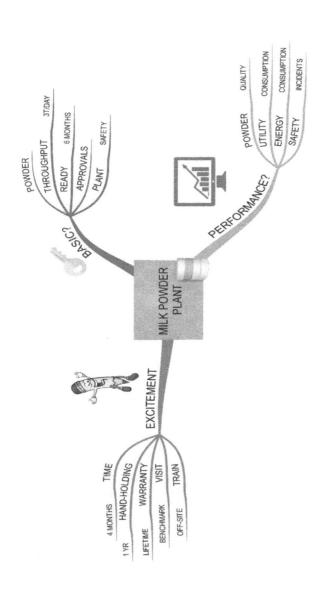

Figure 5.5: *Using Mind Maps to effectively apply Kano's Model for Requirement's Stratification for an engineering project*

A simple Mind Map as shown in figure 5.5 captures these three categories along the three main branches for an engineering-procurement-construction project for milk powder production. The basic factors are the ones' which when missed in the product will cause dissatisfaction to the point of customer not accepting the product. When available, however, it does not cause any significant increase in the customer satisfaction. As shown in figure 5.5, the basic factor for the milk powder plant is first the powder itself. Additionally, the plant throughput, its timeline, certain project approvals, safety factors, would also fall under this category. The performance factors are those which when improved cause a corresponding linear increase in the customer satisfaction. In context of our example, these could be the powder quality, utility consumption, energy consumption etc. Finally, we have the excitement factors which when not present have minimal impact on the customer - but when provided - will delight the customer more than the basic and performance factors. Again for the powder plant, this could include an unexpected early delivery, free handholding for an extended period beyond the plant commissioning, lifetime warranty on some equipment, customer visits and training at similar world class facilities etc.

This Mind Map helps distribute the requirements on one of the three branches, and then maximize opportunities for excitement factors without compromising on the project triple constraints. Again a team approach to this would be extremely fruitful. With all the requirements visually laid out, it becomes easy for the project team to understand which requirements to focus on as the project progresses. A final word of caution in this approach is that over time as more and more companies offer the same thing and customer awareness grows, the excitement factors of today will migrate down to basic factor [20]. It is hence of utmost importance for an organisation to have a formal process in place to keep on identifying excitement factors along the product life cycle.

e)   SCOPE DEFINITION

As per PMBOK [3], project scope management includes processes required to ensure that the project includes all the work required and only the work required to complete the project successfully.

Thus the project scope is the enabler or the set of activities, which lead to the end result i.e. the product or service being created. Once the requirements have been collected and prioritized, the project scope helps identify and integrate the activities to be performed leading to the creation of a Work Breakdown Structure (WBS), which is the basic input for defining the project plan. Having an approved Project Scope early in the project helps reduce the changes and iteration as the project progresses.

A Mind Map helps create a WBS where the chances of missing out a work packet are minimized. Additionally, when this is done as a team exercise, it can be very engaging for all the stakeholders involved. An example of a WBS for a setting up a new production plant is given in figure 5.6. Each of the branches are roughly organized along the timeline of the project and the sub-branches primarily represent the deliverable for that phase. So the first branch is about necessary approvals comprising both internal approvals

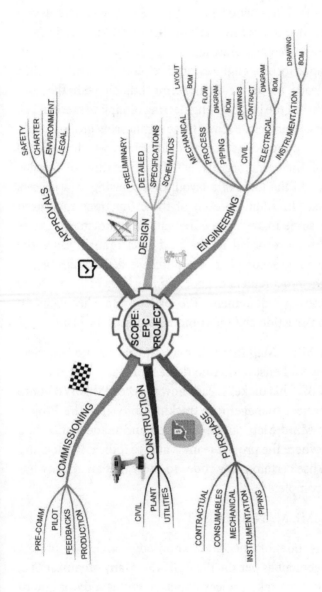

Figure 5.6: *Mind Map capturing the Project Scope for an Engineering-Procurement-Construction (EPC) Project*

such as an approved project charter and also external approvals like environment, legal, safety etc. The design branch has the preliminary design as the first deliverable and the schematic drawings as the final one, which forms the input for the engineering disciplines to work further. This leads us to the Engineering branch with the sub-branches of the involved engineering discipline mechanical, process, piping etc. Each of these engineering groups would in turn be providing a set of deliverables, which mark the end of their engineering activity. Thus this deliverable may be in the form of a layout or a drawing or a process flow etc. In addition, each of these functions may need either some material procurement or contractual services or both as recorded in the next level branch. Once the engineering is complete, the purchase department begins with the procurement of goods and services in line with the engineering requirement. The last two branches focus on the construction and the commissioning of the plant.

A Mind Map like this made involving the complete team would ensure that no deliverables are missed out in the WBS. This makes it easy now to record this WBS onto any project management tracking software. The Project Scope Mind Map can be enlarged and made visible in a place where the project team is able to look at it often and could use certain color codes to show that an activity has been completed.

f) TIME MANAGEMENT

This is one of the nine knowledge areas of project management as per the PMBOK [3]. Many organizations, however, mistake project management as a discipline to manage only the project time line.

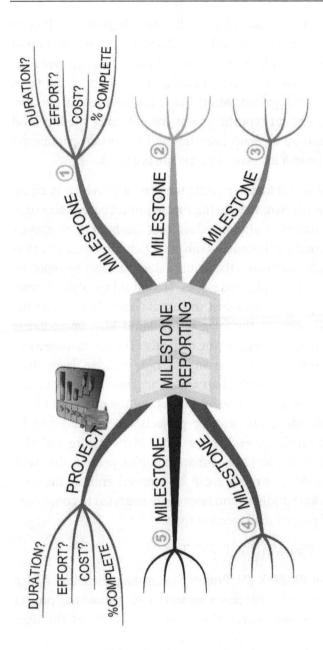

***Figure 5.7:** Mind Map template for top level Milestone Reporting*

Time management is an important Project Management Area and should not be seen in isolation of other equally important areas of Project Management such as risk management, communication planning and team skill development. Mind Maps can be used as effective management reporting tools for outlining the top level milestones as main branches and important parameters for the specific project as the sub branches.

A Mind Map reporting template is provided in figure 5.7. As shown, specific important project parameters such as Milestone duration, effort, cost can be tracked against each of the milestones as sub branches. Subsequently as the project progresses, the actual values can also be reported alongside the planned values. The advantage of this format for reporting as against the usual Gantt chart is that the information in the form of the Mind Map immediately intrigues and engages the audience. The top management may not be keen or having the time to delve deeper into subtasks of a Gantt chart and hence this simple reporting format is quite powerful for getting the attention of the stakeholders. For simpler projects the tracking can be done on the project scope Mind Maps (figure 5.6) also whereas in the case of more complex project, the work break down structure can be mapped entirely on tools such as iMindMap and later easily migrated to commonly used project management tools.

g) COST MANAGEMENT

As per PMBOK [3], Project Cost management knowledge area includes processes necessary to ensure the project is completed within the approved budget. At the time

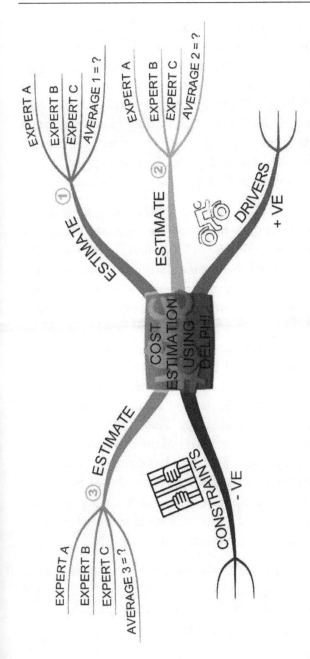

Figure 5.8: Using Mind Maps to capture the Delphi process for Estimating Project Cost

of project initiation, the focus is on having an accurate cost estimation, which would later help in budget control as the project progresses further. One of the techniques used effectively for cost estimation of a complete project is the Delphi. The Delphi process starts with a coordinator explaining in detail the scope of the project to a group of experts in the project domain. The experts are isolated from each other and the coordinator requests a first estimate from the each of the experts individually.

The coordinator can use a Mind Map template as shown in figure 5.8 to record the estimate from each expert on the sub-branch of round 1 estimate. The average is calculated and shared with all the experts. The experts then give a second estimate based on the average that has been shared with them. This time, however, each expert also has to communicate (in writing) individually with the coordinator giving the reasons why their second cost estimate is higher (i.e. project constraints) or lower (i.e. project drivers) than the average shared from the first round. The coordinator records these on the drivers/constraints branch and shares them with all the experts without identifying the author of the drivers/constraints. Then the coordinator asks for a last estimate from all the experts and the average of this final round of estimation is the estimate for the project. Thus on a single page Mind Map the complete Delphi exercise is recorded for easy reference later in the project.

A Mind Map can also be used for identifying all the cost elements at the project start once the major cost heads are identified on the main branches such as employees cost, sub-contractors, equipment cost,

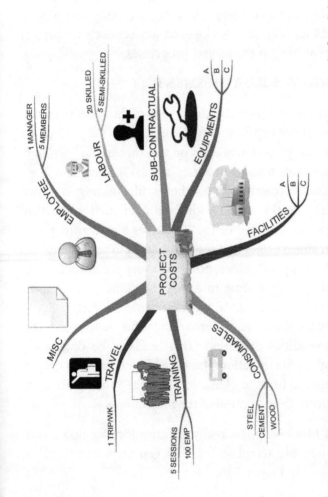

Figure 5.9: *Mind Map to enable identification of all the Cost Elements of a project before initiating detailed estimation*

facilities cost, consumables, trainings, travel etc. A Mind Map template for enabling this is given in figure 5.9. The cost elements thus identified along with the team can be further estimated using the various costing techniques. This Mind Map can also be used subsequently for project cost reporting as the project progresses.

h) TEAM SKILL ASSESSMENT

An area often ignored is the review of the team strengths and weakness upfront before the start of the project. At times the project manager or the owner may wrongly assume that since a previous similar project has been executed successfully, no other skill building is hence required by the team. Additionally, in such a situation the Project Manager or the Resources Manager may also assign similar roles and responsibilities to team members as the last project. Since, however, every project is unique, spending a little time to assess the skills necessary for the project versus those available can really help identify skill gaps, if any, and thereby allow for better roles and responsibilities definition. This needs to be done early enough in the initiation phase itself to prepare the Project manager upfront to plan and fill in the missing skills for the successful execution of the project.

A Mind Map is a really effective tool for doing this. One possible template for skill gap assessment [12] is indicated in Figure 5.10.

The right side of the map captures the skills required for the successful execution of the project- what are the soft skills, such as Project Management, Communication, Negotiation etc., essential for this project and hard skills

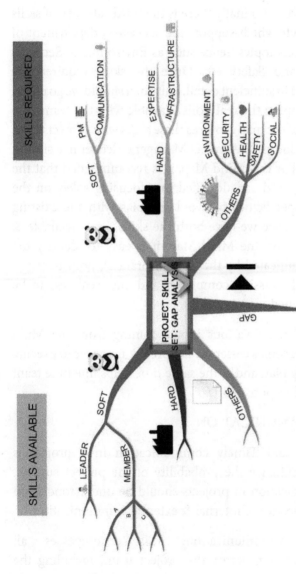

Figure 5.10: *Mind Map template to do a Skill Set Gap Analysis*

could be those based on specific expertise along the project life cycle or specific infrastructure/equipment necessary for the project. Finally there is the third category of skills on subjects which support the successful deployment of the project- topics hence such as Environment, Security, Health, and Safety etc. Once the skills required are identified in sufficient detail, only then should we go ahead with mapping the real skills available with the team. The left side of the map captures these skills with respect to the team, including the Project Manager or leader in a similar fashion. For this Mind Map, it is recommended that the skills required are identified first focusing solely on the project specificities to avoid any bias with the existing skill set. Once we have both the skills, i.e. - available & required - on the Mind Map, it is easy to identify the gap (as indicated by the bottom branch), both in terms of what is missing completely and any weakness to be strengthened.

With these various inputs coming from the Mind Map, it becomes easier for the project manager to execute a training plan and at the same time helps fine tune team roles and responsibilities.

i)   COMMUNICATION

Effective and Timely communication in a project is vital to enhance the probability of the project success. Communication in projects should be understood from the perspective of internal & external communication.

Internal Communication: This encompasses all communication across the project team, including the management or sponsors of the project. The keywords for all internal communication are transparency and a sense of urgency. Also the project manager and the sponsors should demonstrate a sense of direction as well as care, no matter how tough the going may be. Internal communication is vital for the prompt removal of road blocks and keeping the team together at all times.

External Communication: On the other hand, external communication implies communication with the external stakeholders, especially the customer or the end user of the product or service. The keywords for all external communication are branding, supporting and tact. Every project holds the potential for many more projects to come from the same client. External communication - both formal and informal - slowly builds an image in the customer's mind about the project organization. It is hence important that the project staff be trained to communicate in a way that showcases the strength of the organization, indicates continuous support, demonstrates a listening attitude, and above all, is positive and balanced.

It is important to be aware about the above subtle differences between of internal and external communication, even though both finally are a means to the success of the project.

The plans and tools for communication need to integrate both the internal and external aspects. Project communication should be seen as a strategic "resource" for the success of the project and Mind Map is the strategic tool for defining the overall communications need of the project. Communicating the project vision and defining a communication plan are two important elements to be addressed from a communication perspective at the start of the project itself.

Let's see how we can apply Mind Maps for addressing these two important elements.

Communicating the Project Vision: A Mind Map template for developing a project vision was shared in the last chapter (figure 4.1). Let's look with an example, how this Mind Map can be modified for using it as a medium to communicate the project vision. Let's take an example of a housing project. The project is about building a housing complex and the big picture needs to be communicated to the team. A sample Mind Map capturing this is shared in figure 5.11.The first branch of this Mind Map captures the top-level "Why" of the project. The project is being done to fulfill an identified existing need for high end, exclusive and luxurious apartments. These keywords are hence captured on the branch. It is also advisable to include a slogan or a punch line, if any, for the project, which reflects the character of the project, e.g., "Home" Not "Residence" in this case.

The next branch focuses on detailing the "What" to a level that the project team involved is actually able to visualize the same with ease with tangible facts. Depending on the nature of the project, a branch may be necessary to show pre-approvals required, such as those from environmental or other local authorities.

Sometimes further detailing of the "What" branch could help develop an even stronger vision. In the housing project, for example, we find that at the core of the project

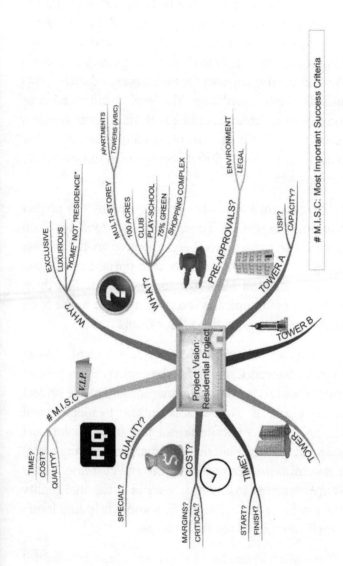

Figure 5.11: Using Mind Maps to Communicate a Project Vision

are the three towers A, B and C. Thus a branch for each the towers would help capture the facts and offerings for the individual towers. As an example, the USP for one of the towers could be the proximity to the club and for another it could be the proximity to the shopping complex. Details about the housing capacity for each tower and such points could also be reflected here. The level of information in these three branches should be such that the uniqueness of each tower becomes evident, making it easier for the project team to see the differences between the seemingly similar towers.

The next three branches are inspired by the project constraint triangle of Time, Cost and Quality. Even though these would have been captured in the project charter, it is good to reiterate these important constraints again in this Mind Map. The top level clarity on these parameters communicates the right message to the team on the expectations on these three fronts.

Finally, we have the M.I.S.C branch, which is "Most Important Success Criteria" for the project. Every project is unique and so is every customer for whom the project is being executed. Thus it is important to identify and visualize the success criteria not just from an internal standpoint (which could be profit margins in many cases) but also from the perspective of the end customer. Is the customer sensitive to timely delivery or to the final quality of the product or the costing? This would help find levers to satisfy or even delight the customer.

The Project Vision Mind Map is an extremely powerful tool to motivate, engage and energize the complete team towards the end result of the project.

Defining a communication plan: Clarity on the Project Manager and the team's roles and responsibilities does not necessarily imply a similar clarity on the project communication aspect. Communication has to be both effective and efficient. As per PMBOK [3], effective communication means that information is provided in the right format, at the right time, to the right audience, and with the right impact whereas efficient communication means providing only the information that is needed. Figure 4.2 in chapter 4 provides a Mind Map to capture all the elements of communication in a project. For complex projects, a communication needs analysis is helpful before drafting a final communication plan. An example of such a Communication Needs Analysis is given in figure 5.12.

In all projects there are some common needs for multiple stakeholders. These are captured in the first branch with the reference "TQC" (Time-Quality-Cost). This would include an approved set of the triple constraints of project schedule, budget and the requirements with the help of specific documents, such as requirement documents etc. The subsequent main branches determine the needs from the perspective of each of the stakeholder. Customer communication needs are identified next. In addition to the "TQC" branch, there could be project events, which the customer would like to be informed about. These could include delays, budget overruns, important milestones and any change in scope initiated by the project team. Similarly in the next branch from the team's perspective the needs could include issues (technical, resource related or others), scope changes and triggered risks and opportunities.

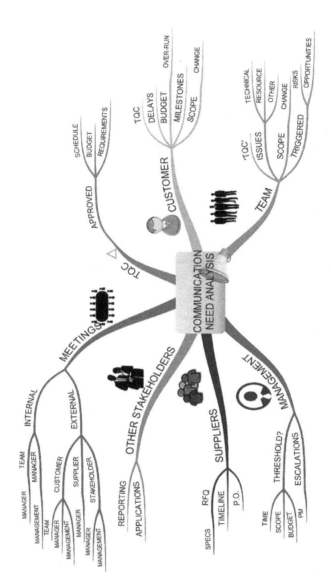

Figure 5.12: *Stakeholders Communication Need Analysis*

These must be reported in a timely manner to everyone in the team. An effective and efficient communication of risks and opportunities would help immensely in keeping the project under control.

The project manager would have similar needs as the project team but additionally he needs to recognize individuals along the project life-cycle. In the hurry to execute the project we may forget the importance of recognition, which is undoubtedly the most powerful form of communication though many times underutilized. Celebrations should not be relegated only towards the end of the project but should be there also at the time of important milestones and successes during the project, especially when projects are of long durations. Thus a main branch for the Project Manager (not shown in Figure) can also be included to identify the recognition/celebration opportunities.

The next branch focuses on the management. The management needs to know about issues, which are impacting the project beyond some set thresholds of time, budget or scope. In addition, the management should be ensured a timely escalation of issues where the Project Manager may need support from them. The suppliers are captured on the next branch with communications needs relating to a RFQ (request for quote) with clear specifications. They should have a formal purchase order and visibility on the timeline within which they need to supply their services or products. Finally, there could be other stakeholders, such as legal or regulatory authorities, who require either regular or one time reporting on issues, such as environmental or health/safety in context of the project.

Once the needs of all the stakeholders have been identified, it is good subsequently to list the possible internal and external meetings (or reports) along with the frequency. Finally, a quick check should be done to see if all the stated communication needs of the stakeholders are being addressed by one or the other identified meets (or reports)?

The project manager should take the primary responsibility for doing a Communication Needs Analysis taking inputs from all the stakeholders. Being sure that no communication need has been left out is an important success factor for the project.

j) OPPORTUNITIES & RISK MANAGEMENT

Traditionally Project management practices have focused a lot on risk management, i.e., on scenarios, which could derail a project. In *"GRASP the Solution"* [2], Chris Griffiths refers to the aspect of Selective Thinking of the mind. He explains that generally speaking the human tendency is to favor information that confirms an existing belief or preconception regardless of whether the information is true or not. For many decades Project Management has formally addressed risks only missing out completely on opportunities to benefit the project. Many project managers have been trained to "selectively" look for risks only during the course of the project, thus becoming blind to opportunities that could positively influence the project outcome.

First and foremost, therefore, we need to rename "Risk Management" "Opportunities & Risk Management" to have a balanced vision of both the aspects.

The PMBOK [3] Guide identifies Project Risk Management to include the processes of conducting risk management planning, identification, analysis, response planning, and controlling risks on a project. There is a clear recognition that the goal of risk management is to increase the likelihood and impact of positive events and decrease the likelihood and impact of negative events in the project.

It is imperative to identify the opportunities and risks at the time of project initiation itself to be able to manage them properly as the project progresses. The figure 5.13 presents a Mind Map to aid in the identification of opportunities and risks by project milestone. Let's take a closer look at this Mind Map.

The first branch captures generic opportunities and risks applicable to the complete project lifecycle. This would comprise typical risks such as currency fluctuation, resource or machinery unavailability, force majeure conditions, process related, macroeconomic risks, environmental risks etc. Once these are identified, the next branches map the risks and opportunities by milestone. Each of the milestone branches has three sub branches: first for identifying the main deliverables of the milestone, second for risks and a third for opportunities. The scope of each of the three sub branches is limited to the specific milestone that they are associated with. This allows for more focused thinking and hence better identification

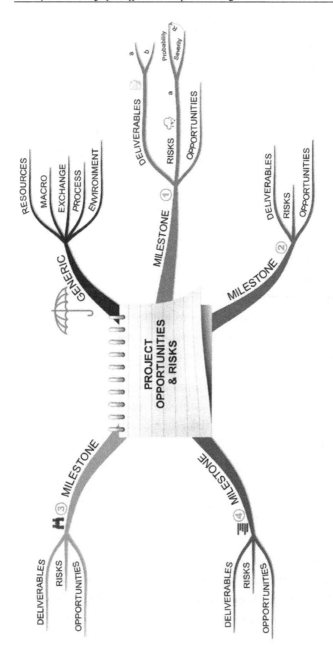

Figure 5.13 *Mind Map to capture Risks & Opportunities by Milestones*

of opportunities and risks. The branches further from the Opportunities and Risks are used for prioritization of the opportunities and risks by assessing their severity and probability using a risk matrix. Just by looking at the number of risks or opportunities identified in each milestone, it would be easy to identify the most risky phase of the project and the one with maximum possible opportunities. We will go into details of quantification of risks in the next chapter on project execution.

There are two ways to use this map. For simpler projects, the complete opportunities and risk identification as well as prioritization could be done on this map itself. Whereas for more complex projects, it could be used for exhaustive identification of opportunities and risks, which are subsequently translated into a risk register. We would cover this in our next chapter.

The start of any project is a strategic decision and giving it sound foundations demands focus and effort. We should proceed with a project only when we have a certain threshold clarity and when we are able to integrate the initial disconnected pieces of information to inspire us towards an end goal. Mind Map is a wonderful tool to give us a holistic view of the project by connecting the scattered and sometimes sketchy pieces of information available at the initiation phase. The various Mind Maps at project initiation help give us the confidence to move ahead with the project and fulfil the promise of the future. Last but definitely not the least should we forget that every project is a wonderful opportunity to build new relationships, which would well go beyond the timeline of the project. With that, our project takes birth and it is time to nurture the small baby to its full human potential.

Chapter 6

The Busy Life: Project Execution

"Execution is a specific set of behaviors and techniques that companies need to master in order to have competitive advantage. It's a discipline of its own."
- Ram Charan and Larry Bossidy, Execution

The execution phase of the project is a bridge between the start, from nebulous thoughts, to the end i.e. the desired product or service. As we proceed deeper into execution, the "cloud of ideas" starts taking shape and an increased clarity of the end goal acts as a wonderful motivational fuel.

The execution phase of a project is akin an adolescent becoming a young adult- full of energy, and more importantly, having clearer direction, which makes for a winning life and project. During the execution phase, activities are intense and hence the rate of consumption of resources is the maximum during this period in comparison to other phases of the project. The keywords in this phase, in addition to execution, are monitoring, reporting, control and risk management.

There is no area of Project Management, which remains untouched during project execution and there are innumerable opportunities for using Mind Maps. Visibility and transparency are central in this phase of the project when hundreds of decisions are being taken using available facts and figures. Mind Maps offer that vital help for capturing all relevant data and allow for easy and quick communication of the same to a large audience in an engaging manner. In this chapter, we look at the opportunities for Mind Mapping across the following important areas for project execution:

- Managing Relations and Communications
- Scope Management
- Time Management
- Cost Management
- Quality Management
- Risk & Opportunities Management
- Procurement Management

Managing Relations & Communications

Communication is the ingredient, which can make or break relations, and hence in projects or for that matter in general in life, we need to talk of Communications & Relations in the same breath. Every communication opportunity is a means of strengthening the partnership with project stakeholders to meet the desired outcome. Let's look at the different important means of communications during projects and how Mind Maps can help in each of the areas:

a) *Teleconferencing*: With an increasing number of projects having multi-locational teams, this means of communication has already gained a

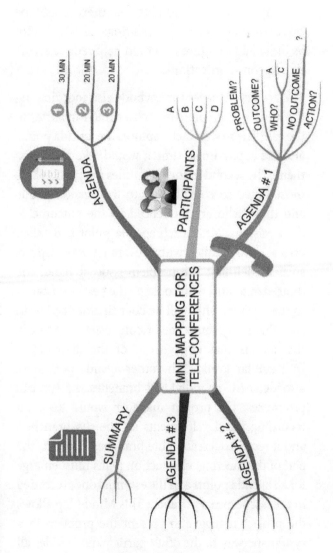

Figure 6.1: *Using Mind Mapping for Preparing and Conducting a Teleconference*

lot in importance in all projects. Many a times though when people from different cultures come participate in a teleconference, there could be possibilities of misunderstandings. A Mind Map as indicated in figure 6.1 could help reduce errors due to communications.

The project manager (or anybody else coordinating the meeting) can prepare such a Mind Map prior to the call. The first branch captures the agenda points and the approximate time it would take to discuss them. The second branch identifies the participants most suited to contributing to the agenda points and those who are influenced by the outcome of the decisions. Next, each agenda point is detailed on a separate branch with sub-branches on aspects such as defining the problem/issue at hand, the desired outcome, who could be the best contributor to the agenda, what will be coordinator's action in case there is no outcome or conclusion and finally the actions that emerge out of the discussions. In a similar fashion, the other agenda points are also detailed on individual branches. As the call progresses, the project manager would keep on recording the developments on the sub-branches, and if required, create more branches. Towards the end of the meeting, clear action plans must emerge for all agenda points and the essential one's recorded in the last summary branch. This Mind Map allows the project manager to present the problem in a systematic way to the other participants besides all inputs received during the call can be very easily plugged into the existing Mind Map. Mind Maps can also be used for an unplanned call where a prior

Mind Map does not exist. In such a situation, instead of taking notes in a linear fashion, start jotting notes in the form of a Mind Map to immediately understand the dimensions and association of the issue/problem. Mind Mapping for note taking is not only fun and engaging but almost instantly makes you a better listener.

b) *Project Meetings:* In today's world of technology, the line between virtual and physical meetings is diminishing though physical meetings do retain an edge in terms of impact or effectiveness. Mind Maps are being very effectively used for brainstorming and conflict resolution in meetings. Let's look at these two areas from a "Mind Mapping" perspective.

- *Brainstorming:* A large amount of literature is available on this subject in the public domain. Majority of organizations are either not practicing brainstorming at all or doing a poor job of this powerful technique. In *"GRASP the Solution"* [2], the authors suggest that for brainstorming to be successful, it needs to be a proactive and purposeful activity, and the best results come in when both the individual and group creativity is leveraged in a carefully managed process. They recommend Mind Map to record, develop and arrange ideas. In contrast to traditional brainstorming, the problem is first addressed at the individual level with each individual making his/her own Mind Map of the issue to be tackled. Subsequently the team comes together to stitch all the

Mind maps together to create a bigger Mind Map. This ensures that a larger pool of ideas is generated than through traditional group brainstorming. This idea pool is then optimized with a process of filtering the ideas to identify the best solution. In Project Management, brainstorming is a must for tackling seemingly difficult issues, either technical or otherwise, for finding optimized solutions for perceived/real risks, and in general, for overcoming any seemingly impossible road blocks during the project lifecycle. There will be opportunities aplenty for using Mind Maps.

- *Conflict Resolution:* With multiple stakeholders and personalities in a team, situations involving conflict do arise as we move to the end line of the project. Negotiation is the communication process that helps resolve a conflict and allows the involved parties to come to a mutual agreement. Tony Buzan, in his book *"Mind Maps for Business"* [10] details how Mind Maps can be effectively used in negotiation. He states that the first goal of negotiation is to explore and understand the Mind Map of the person with whom you are negotiating. Secondly, you need to make sure you communicate your Mind Map, the map of your territory to the person with whom you are negotiating. And finally the negotiation process should converge with a "melding" of the two Mind Maps towards a win-win solution.

  A Mind Map such as the one given in figure 6.2 is useful for conflict resolution.

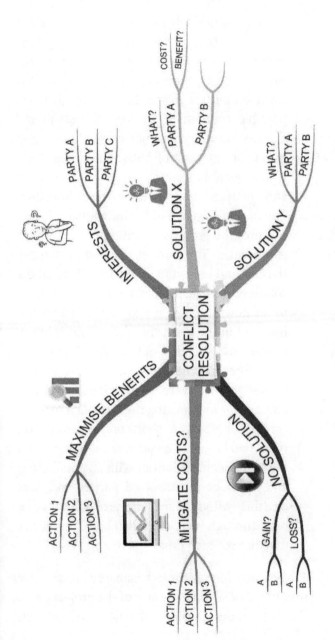

Figure 6.2: *Mind Map to aid Conflict Resolution*

It is particularly powerful if made together with both the parties after they have done some pre-work on the conflicting issue. The first branch captures the clear interests of the involved parties A and B. Let's say that two possible solutions exist, viz, X and Y, and the best solution has to be chosen keeping in mind the interests of both the parties. Each of the possible solutions X and Y is detailed and analyzed in individual main branches. The first sub-branch of the individual solution captures the proposed solution in the "What" sub-branch. The next sub-branches identify the cost and benefit to each party. Once all the solutions are exhausted, the last branch is used to jot down both gain and loss to the parties involved in the event that there is no solution to the issue. Another option would be to use two more branches, one for possible actions to mitigate the various identified costs and another for maximizing the identified benefits across solutions. A short brainstorming on these two branches could give more inputs on the best possible solution. With all possibilities and views of the involved parties laid bare on this Mind Map, the probability of a breakthrough increases when both the parties together see each other's gains and losses.

c) *Project Branding:* A project manager consciously may not choose to be the face of the project given the probabilities attached to the success of a project.

Every project manager, however, must realize that good publicity about the project right from the start certainly helps in enhancing stakeholder engagement thereby improving the probabilities associated with its success. Unless there are some confidentiality concerns about a project, there is no reason why every project should not be highly publicized amongst the stakeholders. Project branding using Mind Maps is fast, clear, compact and an effective way of achieving this. Mind Maps such as the Project Benefits Analysis presented in Chapter 5 (in fig 5.3) can be used effectively not only for branding, motivating but also garnering more support for the project. Aspects such as those relating to the team, viz, it taking pride in their contribution to the project can also be easily incorporated into this Mind Map. Such Mind Maps, which capture the essence of the complete project, should be freely shared with all, displayed at prominent places within the organization and kept updated on a regular basis.

d) *Communicating Emotions*: A project undoubtedly generates a variety of emotions. And a good project manager maximizes opportunities for releasing any pent up emotions before they take explosive dimensions with any negative impact on the project. A simple Mind Map as shown in figure 6.3 could help capture team emotions as the project progresses.

The picture at the center of the Mind Map should preferably represent the project end goal.

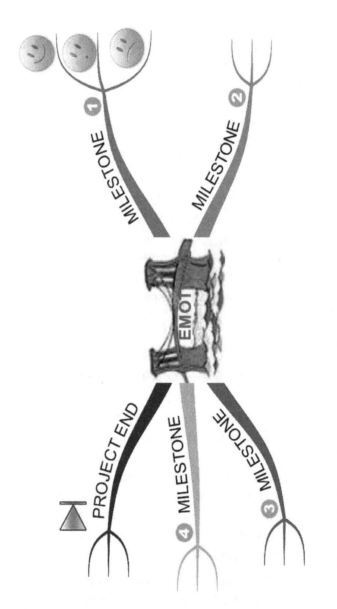

Figure 6.3: *Mind Map to capture and Communicate Emotions during a project lifecycle*

So if the project is about constructing a bridge then a photo of a bridge would become the central picture in such a Mind Map. The project milestones are charted out on each of the branches and there are three sub branches displaying emoticons of *Happy*, *Neutral* and *Sad*. At the end of a project milestone, each team member puts a tick (or duplicates the emoticon) against the emotions, which best represents his feelings in reaching this milestone. The team should also be free to further write or elaborate on their choice of emoticon. If the majority have selected the smiley, then in all probability, things are fine but at the same time, any sad emoticon could be investigated deeper at the discretion of the Project Manager. If there are too many sad emoticons, then the project manager could quickly take stock of the situation through either a one on one meeting or a group meeting.

Scope Management

The Product & Project Scope need to be clearly defined at project initiation. The unavoidable challenges while executing a project are, however, to keep the changes in the Product and Project Scope within an acceptable limit as well as minimizing any negative impact on the key project metrics. A change in the end product's specifications will invariably impact the project scope, however a project scope change (i.e. an addition or deletion of an activity to the Work Breakdown Structure) must not result in deviating the end product's specifications; instead it should reinforce the existing features of the end deliverable.

Either way the challenge would be to correctly assess the impact of the change and subsequently decide to accept or reject it. A quick Mind Map for assessing the change is shown in figure 6.4. The branches on the right of the Mind Map assess the impact of the change on Time, Cost, Quality & any other factor. On the other hand, the impact of not accepting the change may not always mean that the status of the project remains unchanged. Thus the branches on the left of the Mind Map capture the impact on the same set of parameters if the change is not accepted. It is important that each of the factors therein is quantified to the extent possible. On the same map, we also analyze mitigation action if any, for the individual impacts identified on a separate sub-branch. This allows us to investigate possible mitigation actions and their related costs.

Though this process may seem a little obvious, it has two big benefits. First, it systematically helps to avoid missing any impact of the change/no-change by looking at the project constraint (and other) factors one by one. Secondly, it allows for easy communication of the impact analysis in an extremely clear and concise way to all stakeholders involved thus facilitating a quick decision on the project.

Time Management

During project execution, the keyword is control, i.e., ensuring that the project adheres as closely to the project plan as possible. From a time management perspective, the goal would be to control schedule variance in the tasks and milestones of the project. Depending on the project

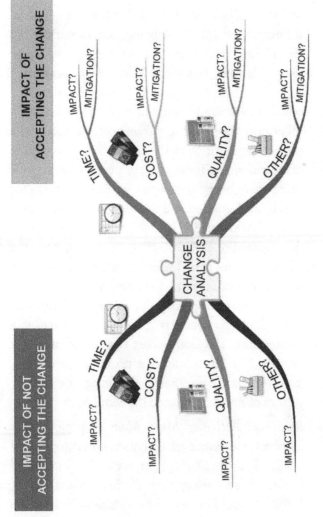

Figure 6.4: *Mind Map for Impact Analysis of a Change to the project*

complexity, duration, resources etc., there are many ways that Mind Maps can be used for monitoring project progress and reporting. Let's look at some of these:

- *Milestone Tracking*: This is a particularly useful technique of Mind Mapping for capturing the big picture and reporting to the management. The milestone reporting Mind Map previously given in Chapter 5 (figure 5.7) under Project Time management would come in handy here. For each milestone, the tracking parameters specific to the project/organization can be used in the sub-branches of the milestone. These could be percentage progress or effort or work completed (in man weeks) etc., which are identified and flashed during the project review board meeting with the customer. As against the conventional Gantt chart representation, the advantage here is that there is an immediate focus on the critical control parameters of the project without worrying about the micro level timeline representation, which is the central essence of a Gantt chart. The Gantt chart is a useful input for creating this Mind Map. The project decisions are, however, finally facilitated capturing the holistic picture of the milestones in the Mind Map.

- *Resources Activities Mind Map*: A project plan involves a number of activities, interlinked and assigned to multiple resources. An integrated project plan using any Project Management software would be useful for getting a view of the complete set of activities and doing what if analysis. From the individual resources perspective, however, there should be clarity on what individual

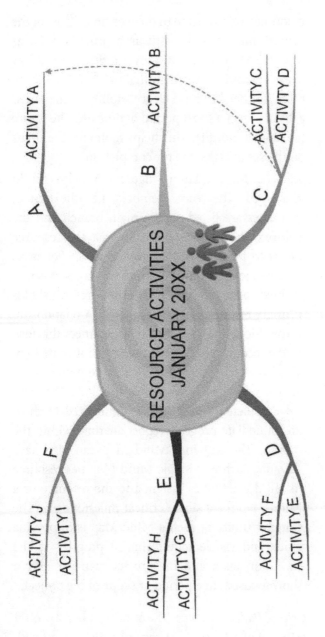

Figure 6.5: *Mind Map to track Individual Resources activities*

resources are expected to do over time. Most of the project management software's provide a linear calendar view of activities over a time period, say over a month. At an individual resource level, there is a need to have clear visibility of the tasks/ activities over a short period of time into the future (at most a month). This helps maintain the focus on the set of tasks due for completion).

The Mind Map in figure 6.5 helps fill in this need. The team members, i.e., the human resources are listed on the main branch and the sub-branches are the activities that the resource needs to perform in the given period. For tasks assigned jointly to two or more resources, it is first defined on the sub-branch of the resource, who holds primary responsibility for the same. A relationship arrow (dotted arrow) then helps connect this task to the second resource required to contribute to it. The Mind Map should preferably be pasted in an area where it becomes visible to all. As the tasks get completed, these can be highlighted to show an immediate progress report anytime within the month. The activities Mind Map can also have variants, such as a single Mind Map per resource for all the activities assigned to the resource or a Mind Map for a single critical milestone etc. The primary utility of such a Mind Map is to provide quick and visible monitoring of progress to the execution team and the project manager over a short focused time period or scope of the project..

- *Critical Path Mind Map*: The critical path in a project is the set of activities that constitute the longest path in the project. The critical path in a project may

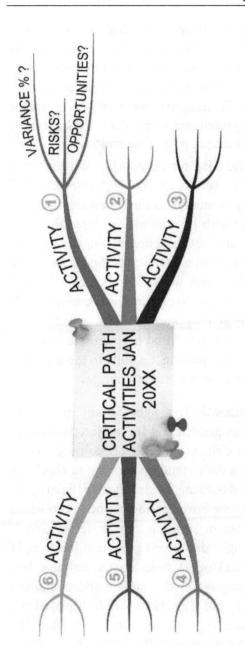

Figure 6.6: Mind Map to Report and Monitor Project Critical Path

change due to a change in the project scope or delays added to the non-critical activities, which eventually may generate a new critical path for the project. Any delay in an activity on the critical path could result in a delay of the complete project. As a good practice many organizations, therefore, continuously monitor the critical path of the project.

A Mind Map for monitoring and reporting the critical path is shown in figure 6.6. This Mind Map is similar to the milestones tracking Mind Map with two differences. First, the main branches are not milestones but the specific activities that make up the critical path. Secondly, in the sub-branch we include branches for risk and opportunities to capture factors, which could derail the activity and enablers, which could help speed up. This Mind Map is useful for both management reporting, visibility to the team and outlining risk with possible strategies.

- *Agile Dashboard*: The Agile Scrum method of Project Management has the Project Dashboard as the core element for the team to review daily. It involves a daily stand up meeting to check the progress and bottlenecks in the goals defined by the team for a time boxed period of one to two weeks (called a Sprint in Agile Scrum terminology). The usual agile dashboard goes from left to right with the backlog of tasks on the extreme left; work in progress in the middle and completed tasks to the right. This dashboard is displayed at a vantage point (usually on a white board) where the complete team can view it anytime. Let's look at

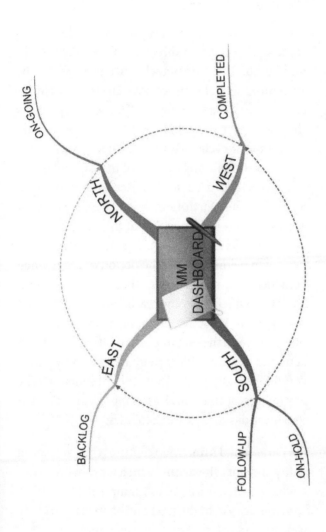

Figure 6.7: *A "Directional" Mind Map for use as a Project Dashboard in Agile Scrum*

how we can effectively use a dashboard in the form of a Mind Map, which can also be referred to as a Directional Mind Map (refer figure 6.7).

The Mind Map has four branches each representing the four directions East, West, North and South. The four branches are inspired by the sun's movement. Let us see how. The sun rises in the east and kick starts a new day. Thus East represents the backlog or the activities, which we plan to do in our sprint cycle. West is the direction in which the Sun sets denoting the end of the day and hence this branch is used to represent the completed activities. The North branch is placed topmost. It represents the noon position of the Sun and hence all active tasks in the sprint are captured here. South lies down below and it is the period of night when activities are minimal. It, therefore, represents activities, which for some reason are on hold or are purely follow up activities requiring minimal effort but are nevertheless important. The follow up activities may eventually result in an activity which could fall in any of the three other branches. The advantages of this Mind Map representation over the linear dashboard are as follows:

⊙ The Directional Mind Map captures time as a spiral reality and not a linear one, which is probably closer to what it is in nature. As an example the transition from one season to the next one happens gradually over the repetition of one day over another.

⊙ In reality in projects, there would always be tasks, which are put on hold and are captured separately in the South branch in the Mind Map. Usually such tasks are not earmarked separately in a Linear Agile Dashboard. The Separate branch with the representation of all the on hold tasks /follow-up tasks allows the PM to keep them in focus and await the right moment to convert these into an action tagged to any of the other branches.

⊙ The radial structure of the dashboard is more engaging for the brain as against the normal linear way of capturing the activities.

The aforestated are a few methods used for tracking activities and milestones with the help of Mind Maps. Reporting and monitoring activities may vary in each Organization but there would plenty of opportunity and advantage for plotting these into Mind Maps.

Cost Management

Cost management is interpreted in different ways in brick and mortar projects as opposed to software development projects. The cost figures are measured directly in monetary terms in construction related projects, whereas in software projects the basic measurement unit is the billable man-hour of effort. The man-hours (or an equivalent unit) are then converted into a monetary figure using a standard conversion factor specific to the project or the organization.

Either ways, project's cost management is an important discipline and let's look at how Mind Maps can help reinforce managing costs in projects.

In the last chapter (fig 5.9), we discussed a Mind Map, which would help identify all the resources for a project.

As indicated in figure 5.9, depending on the nature of the project, the main branches for the project cost head could be human, material, subcontracting and any other (trainings, travel). For projects with a known lifecycle and low complexity, it is easy to identify the costs on a single Mind Map of this nature. Additional sub-branches can be used to display the actual costs alongside the planned costs in the Mind Map of figure 5.8. The complete project cost tracking can be done on a separate branch capturing the cumulative actual/planned costs. Any other cost metric, such as a cost variance, which would help analyze whether the project is running on a budget surplus or deficit can also be introduced in this Mind Map. This Mind Map is a wonderful way to present the big picture with complete clarity to the management as the project progresses, on how the costs are being incurred on various resources and the overall cost variance in the project.

The biggest advantage of using Mind Maps for Cost Management is that it minimizes the risk of missing out on any of the cost elements, and secondly, it generates visually appealing reports easily understood by all stakeholders.

Quality Management

Quality in simple terms implies conforming to requirements first and foremost as specified by the customer and then by the other stakeholders without comprising on the customer requirements. As per PMBOK [3], quality management includes quality planning, control and assurance. Let's look at each of these aspects individually and explore Mind Mapping opportunities therein.

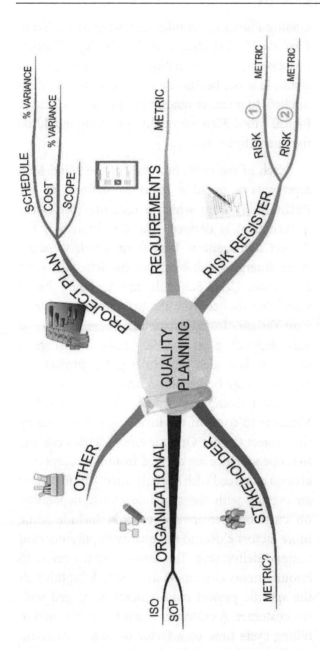

Figure 6.8: *Quality Planning using Mind Maps*

- *Quality Planning:* Jennifer Greene et al. in "*Head First PMP*" [21] state that the Quality Planning process focuses on taking all the information available at the beginning the project and figuring out how to measure quality and prevent defects. A logical Mind Map for quality planning would be the one in figure 6.8.

  Each of the main branches of the Mind Map represents a possible input as defined in the PMBOK [3] from which a measure (preferably quantitative) is derived. The first branch is the Project Management Plan from which we draw three emerging sub-branches on Schedule, Cost and Scope. The Schedule metric could be % schedule variance from the baseline and similarly Cost Variance from the baseline. These again could vary depending on specific needs and interests of the stakeholder, e.g., in a given project the customer may be keener to know the percentage of Project Completion rather that the Schedule Variance to confirm the invoicing being done by the Project Owner Organization. Metrics relating to scope variance are derived from the acceptance criteria as agreed with the customer. This may have an overlap with the schedule metric depending on customer sensitivity or could include some more factors closer to the quality requirements of the end deliverable. The second branch refers to Requirements Documentation, which captures all the specific project requirements as agreed with the customer. A customer wants to cut his current billing cycle time by a factor of 30%. This could translate easily into a quality metric, which the end product would target. The next source could be the Risk Register outlined on a separate branch with the identified risks at the start of the project. Depending on the individual risks, a strategy would be defined which could either be Risk Acceptance or Transfer or Mitigate or Monitor. Specifically Risks with a Monitoring Strategy could result in a metric, which could help identify when a specific mitigation action needs to be defined or executed. The stakeholder register could be another source for identifying specific interests of all the project stakeholders and thereby potentially identifying a quality metric to be tracked. The next branch focuses on Organizational factors, which may result in quality metrics derived from external management system benchmarks or internal standard operating procedures of the organization. The external management system could be standards or certifications (such as ISO) that the organization is bound to comply with. These could be standards for quality, safety, information security or disaster recovery etc. The existing Standard operating Procedures (SOP) of the organization may also prescribe metric measurement over and above those required by an external benchmark standard. Finally it is a good idea to have a branch for any other factor, which does not fall in the previously identified branches. An important Mind Map can also be built using solely the acceptance criteria as defined by the customer. The Mind Map can include branches

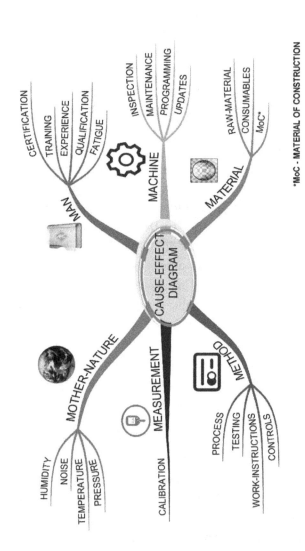

Figure 6.9: Cause Effect Analysis using Mind Maps

capturing various criteria such as Technical, Cost, Non-functional, Timeliness etc. This Mind Map once signed off by the customer can help in sharply focusing on the results as desired by the customer.

- *Quality Control:* As per PMBOK [3], Quality Control is the process of monitoring and recording results of executing the quality activities to assess performance and recommend necessary changes. A number of tools are recommended for quality control, which help investigate possible reasons for poor quality and the corrective action necessary. Imagine an automatic packaging machine installed as part of a bigger project.

  If the packaging machine is not found to be working at its optimum level you may need to investigate the possible cause. A Cause Effect analysis could be done using a Mind Map as shown in figure 6.9 instead of a Fish Bone diagram. The possible cause categories are placed on each main branch of the Mind Map. Applying the 6M principle to an equipment, the branch categories would be:

⊙ *Man*: Possible causes could be related to training, qualifications, experience, certification, fatigue etc.

⊙ *Machine*: Usual causes could be issues relating to maintenance, inspections, programming, software updates etc.

⊙ *Material*: would cover factors such as raw material, consumables, construction material etc.

⊙ *Method*: including factors such as process, testing, work instructions and control etc.

⊙ *Measurement*: such as an error in calibration

⊙ *Mother Nature*: This would cover environmental causes such as noise, humidity, temperature, pressure etc.

Once the various factors are outlined in the Mind Map, a systematic analysis is carried out to identify the factor(s) causing the failure. For Administration or Marketing related problems the 8P analysis can be done wherein each branch of the Mind Map would carry one of the P's, namely,: Product (or service), Price, People, Place, Promotion, Procedures, Processes and Policies. Similarly for the service industry, the Ishikawa diagram can be used analyzing the 5S, i.e., Surrounding, Suppliers, Systems, Skills and Safety.

Quality control boils down to having the right investigative approach for which Mind Maps are very effectively used. Related to this, another technique, which Chris covers in his book *"GRASP the Solution"* [2] is the 5 Wives & 1 Husband, which involves looking at a problem by asking the 6 questions: WHY-WHAT-WHERE-WHEN-WHO and HOW. Each of these questions would be captured on the branch of a Mind Map as shown in figure 6.10 followed by sub-branches capturing the answers to each question.

A similar Mind Map with detailed sub-branches was also shared in figure 4.5 for problem solving. The best way to use this Mind Map is to

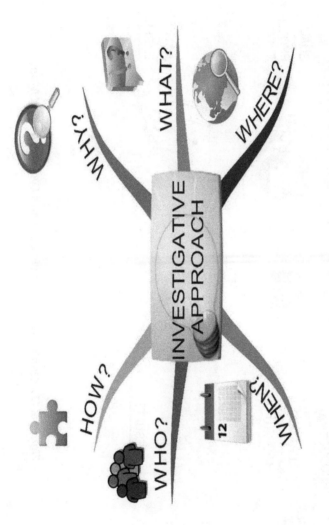

Figure 6.10: *Mind Maps for investigative approach in Quality Control*

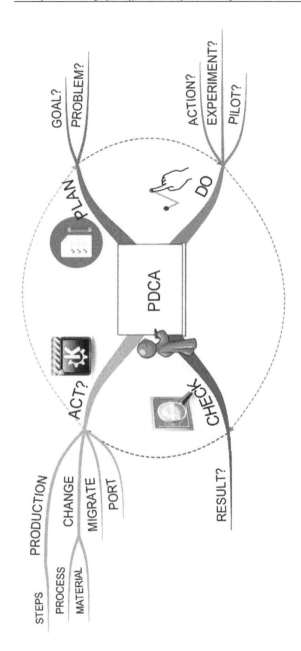

Figure 6.11: *Quality Assurance via Deming's Cycle on a Mind Map*

first draw all the six branches and then answer the questions in a freewheeling way and not in specific order. Preferably this should be done utilizing the brainstorming principles previously stated i.e. starting with the individual and then creating the Mind Map collaboratively, it would more effectively allow a solution or a concrete direction to emerge.

- *Quality Assurance:* The quality assurance process uses the outputs of quality plan and quality control activities to initiate actions necessary for continuous process improvements. Some of the tools used more often for Quality Assurance include Project Auditing, Project Process Analysis and Quality Control Tools.

  One of the most fundamental tools for quality improvement is the Deming's Cycle of Plan-Do-Check-Act or a PDCA cycle. For any quality issue or an improvement program, Mind Maps are quite intuitive for outlining the PDCA cycle. Let's say you have a quality issue in your bottling plant wherein 20% of the bottle caps end up loose as against a snug fit requirement for zero spillage of the bottled liquid. So you start with your Mind Map as indicated in figure 6.11 where the each of the branch represents one element of the PDCA cycle. On the Plan branch, you need to write down your goal or problem statement, which is to reduce the loose caps by a certain percentage. Now your quality planning and control analysis would indicate that the cap needs tapering by 1 mm on the edges. You next decide to implement this on a sample set of caps, which is recorded on the "Do" branch as cycle

1 involving 100 bottles. The "Check" branch would then record the result of this run along with any other specific measure that you would like to keep a tab of. Finally the "Act" branch will list the actions you need to take to incorporate a process change as a result of this or you could decide on another cycle of testing. Multiple cycles of PDCA can easily be incorporated into the Mind Map along with additional details such as timelines and cost.

Risk and Opportunities Management

A weakness that many projects suffer from is the insufficient identification of risks and opportunities. Mind Maps can play a vital role in identification of the risks and opportunities either as through a team brainstorming exercise or attempted individually by a project manager.

A risk or an opportunity is simply an event that could negatively or positively influence the project schedule, cost or quality. Risks are easier to understand since project managers are trained over years in doing this. Opportunity sighting may, however, need some additional focus and practice. Let's look at some examples of opportunities for positive impact on a project. Being able to incorporate an available but unused part or machinery, reduction in government duties, exchange rate fluctuations, fall in the raw materials cost are all examples of cost related opportunities. Finally quality related opportunities could be a technological breakthrough awaited anytime from the research team.

The Mind Map template in figure 6.12 is an example for identifying risks and opportunities categorized as technical, external, organizational risks and any other

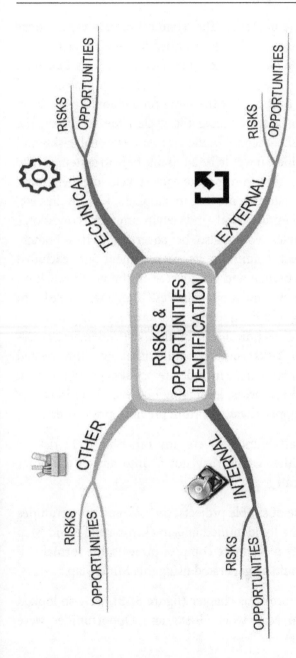

Figure 6.12: *Risk & Opportunities identification using Mind Maps*

on separate branches. The technical branch would focus on challenges and opportunities for achieving the end product quality. For example, factors such as first time usage of a new hardware or software in a project could represent a risk but at the same time it could provide an opportunity for reducing the cycle time for doing the project. The second branch covers external risks and opportunities. It would be advisable here to systematically identify these with respect to each stakeholder, beginning with the customer, moving to suppliers, legal bodies etc. Macroeconomic/social and environmental conditions, if applicable, would also be covered on this branch. The project team and its management are excluded from this branch and get covered in the next branch on internal risks and opportunities. The internal risks to projects would include organizational risks like resource availability, technical capabilities, dependencies, cross-functional risks, multicultural risks etc. The related opportunities could include items like possibilities of additional resources, leveraging on tasks done in earlier project, supplies available from previous projects etc.

The last branch covers any other possible risk or opportunities, which may not fit into any of the other previous categories.

In case of simple projects, the risk and opportunities can be broadly identified and tracked on the Mind Map itself whereas for more complex projects, the formal risk register could be generated using this Mind Map.

In the previous chapter (figure 5.13), we also looked at a Mind Map where Risks and Opportunities were identified by milestones. On this Mind Map itself, sub-branches can be drawn from the identified risks to capture the severity of the risk and its probability on a scale of either one to three or one to 10 (where one represents the low severity or low probability). The risk priority number, which is the multiplication of the quantified severity and probability, can also be included in the Mind Map for prioritizing the identified risks. Depending on the scale being used (for quantifying severity and probability), any risk greater than and/ or equal to a threshold risk should have a conscious risk strategy associated with it.

Procurement Management

Project Procurement management includes activities required for procuring services or products from outside the organization. Depending on the nature of the organization, the procurement activity may be a substantial part of the project, such as Engineering, Procurement and Construction Projects. On the other hand, certain software development projects can be done with minimal procurements. In general, whereas procurement activities are substantial in brick and mortar projects, these are usually limited in case of pure software projects.

Mind Maps are quite useful for creating a top level Bill of Material for products to be delivered. As an example, if a house is to be built then the construction materials required could be captured on a Mind Map as shown in Figure 6.13. The sub-branches could be consumables, electrical, woodwork, plumbing and finishing items. Some of the items could be estimated using some thumb

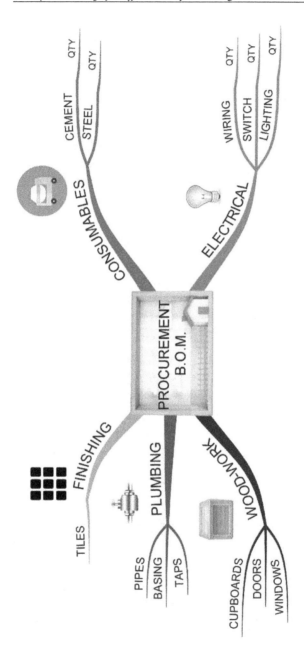

Figure 6.13: *Managing Procurement using Mind Maps*

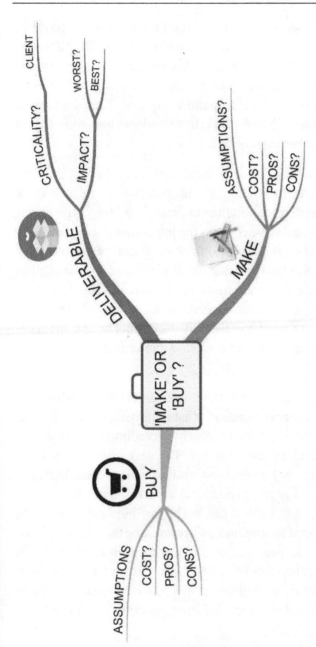

Figure 6.14: *"Make" or "Buy" Decision using Mind Maps*

rules based on the size of the house and there could be other items, which may need to be actually calculated based on the design of the house such as the woodwork. The sub -branches can be accordingly selected to aid a good estimate of the quantity required. The advantage of using such a Mind Map is that it reduces the probability of missing out on any item.

Another dilemma faced very often during projects, especially in relation to sub-contracting an activity, is the question of whether to "make" or "buy". The choice is between whether to do the job within the organization using the available resources or to outsource to a third party. A simple decision Mind Map such as the one given in figure 6.14 can come to the rescue. The first main branch answers some questions about the deliverable for which we need to take this decision. The sub-branches answer questions like what is the critical aspect of the product for the client?

What is the worst possible impact if the deliverable misses the specification? What is the best possible leverage or benefit that we can expect by exceeding the specification as desired by the customer. The next branches focus on the make or buy decision, and for either of the decisions, we would analyze additional aspects. First, what are the assumptions behind the "make" or "buy" decision? With these set of assumptions, what would be the costs involved? Finally the pros and cons of the decision are recorded in the next two sub-branches. Once this landscape has been completed, it would enable a better decision in light of the available facts and information captured on this Mind Map.

We have seen in this chapter that there are a number of opportunities for using Mind Maps during the execution phase. The execution phase requires focused actions, which are continuously aligned to the big picture of the project from the start to the end. Mind Maps are extremely useful for capturing a holistic picture of the project, which easily allow further drilling into the micro aspects.

A number of critical decisions are taken during the execution phase of the project, which directly influence the successful outcome of the project. Mind Maps not only help unleash creativity in decision making but also break complex problems into solvable chunks.

Last but not the least, the execution phase demands a strong collaboration to successfully and creatively deliver the project. The process of Mind Mapping, specially when attempting as a group, is a great integrator of not only ideas but also individuals by creatively engaging everyone to give their best. Utilizing Mind Maps frequently for project meets is really beneficial for generating a positive team spirit.

We look at how Mind Mapping can aid an effective formal project closure in the next chapter.

CHAPTER 7

The Project End: Doorway to a New Beginning

"A good completion takes a long time; a bad completion cannot be changed later." — Zhuangzi, The Complete Works of Chuang Tzu

We are never the same person at the end of the project as we were at its beginning and being conscious about this change can magnify our learning manifold. The focus of all the tools during this project closing phase is to enable a reflection on what went well and what could have been done better.

The last phase of a project is similar to our sunset years. After the hectic execution phase, there is a slowdown followed with complete closure of all the project activities. The consumption, if any, of material resources and the human effort is the least and eventually falls to zero on project closure. It is a good time for reflection on the learnings from the project, irrespective of the final outcome. All projects are good as long as we have learn something from them, technical, soft skills or any other aspect.

WHY & WHEN TO CLOSE A PROJECT?

Just as a man has the potential to live a fully healthy life, similarly all projects start with the promise of delivering a satisfying product or a service to a stakeholder. At the same time, we need to accept that a certain percentage of projects in a company's portfolio would be aborted before their expected conclusion. This could be due to a number of reasons internal or external to the project organization.

A successful project results in a service or product delivery to the customer with a positive cash flow for the project organization. This would entail customer acceptance of the project requirements and receiving all project payments against the raised invoices. The management of the project organization should formally announce the project closure so that the project manager can start the closure activities.

On the other hand, many a times projects end midway due to multiple reasons ranging from product technical failure, lack of resources, relevance of the project scope to legal or regulatory issues, macro-economic factors etc. Depending on the reasons for closure, the management may not always be transparent about it. There is a natural urgency within the organizations management to move away quickly from the failed project, not realizing that sometimes these failures offer accelerated and valuable learnings. In such a situation, the first priority of the Project manager would be to get complete visibility on why the project was aborted or stalled. Next he should try to get a formal closure note from the management. Even when the management resists putting it on record but there is sufficient clarity that the project is no longer viable, the project manager at his level should formalize the closure within his project team.

Either ways, a formal project closure is necessary to conduct-- this is not an option but a mandatory phase for any project, irrespective of the final outcome of the project. This is often neglected in projects and when missed many times over, it may nurture a quiet discontent amongst the team members, which otherwise could have been systematically addressed.

Few reasons why a formal closure for projects is a must:

a) The project resources, both human as well as material, need to be released for other projects;

b) To formally capture what went well in the project;

c) To understand from the team what can be further improved and release pent up feelings, if any;

d) To capture creative ideas, which need to be formally protected either through a patent, trade secret or used for publicity through a publication;

e) To recognize the effort of the team members and celebrate;

f) Finally, just as the brain generally tends towards completeness, similarly when a project is formally closed, it gives a sense of satisfaction and fulfillment.

Given these reasons, it is not difficult to see the benefits of a formal project closure meet to enhance team maturity for handling future projects.

HOW TO CLOSE A PROJECT?

There are three distinct phases that need to be addressed to draw maximum benefits from a project closure meet. These are:

(i) *Pre Closure Meet activities:* The Project Manager holds the prime responsibility to ensure good preparation before the closure meet. In the event of an unexpected project closure, he would need to have full clarity on "why" the closure. Organizations practicing formal project closure normally do so using a project closure checklist to aid the Project Manager. There are essentially two aspects to address during closure. First, to reassess that there are no (or minimal) pending items, which could, from a project management perspective, disqualify the project from being formally closed. The second, and possibly more importantly, the purpose of the checklist is to identify learnings from the project. While the usual approach is to get these filled in the form of a linear checklist, this could be done more creatively using a Mind Maps.

A proposed Mind Map template for pending items is shown in figure 7.1. The first branch questions if there are any pending project requirements for fulfillment.

In case of there being a few pending requirements and assuming these do not seriously hinder the project closure, actions are then identified with Who-What-When for achieving the requirements. The next branch identifies pending activities with reference to the project documentation. The records and documents

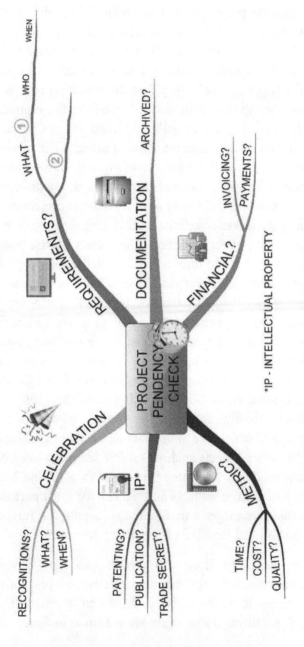

Figure 7.1: Project Pendency Checklist using Mind Maps

from the project should be archived logically in line with the company standard operating procedures. Financial closure is another important aspect to be checked for both with respect to the customer and the supplier. For example, is the invoicing complete or have all the payments been made to the supplier? The project metrics with respect to Time, Cost and Quality are captured on the next branch. The metrics reflect how well the project was managed. New ideas invariably get generated during projects within the organization and it may be likely that the project team may have overlooked the same during the travails and stress of project execution. The project closure phase is an opportune time to revisit intellectual property and/or ideas generated and assess if any of these need protection through patenting, publication, trade secret etc. This important intellectual property generated and the strategy associated with it is outlined on the next branch. The last branch focuses on celebration, which includes team as well as individual recognition and Who-What-When planning for it. These different items broadly cover all the closure aspects of the project, which are more factual in nature whereas the softer aspects such as project learnings are best captured on a separate Mind Map. As this Mind Map is based more on facts and figures, for most part the Project manager can fill in the details for further sharing and for inputs from the project team.

Learnings from the project can play a very important role for future corrective or preventive actions. It is, therefore, preferred to approach this subject through a separate Mind Map as in figure 7.2.

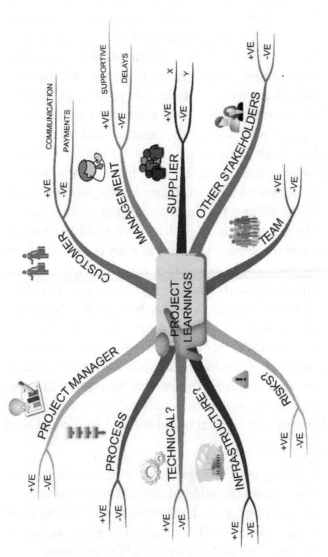

Figure 7.2: *Mind Map to capture Project Learnings*

As part of the preparation for the closure meet, the Project Manager could keep this template (fig 7.2) ready for enabling a brainstorming on learnings. Each of the main branches focuses on a specific aspect of the project, which includes customer, management, supplier, team, other stakeholders, risks, Infrastructure, technical, process and project manager. For each of these aspects, the sub-branches capture what went well (positive) and what could have been done better (negative). As an example, "open communication" may have been a *positive* aspect vis-à-vis the customer but the *negative* could be the delayed payments against the invoices raised. The management might have been visibly supportive about the project, but delay in a few critical decisions by them could have had a negative impact on the project. Similarly amongst suppliers, there could be a particular supplier, who may have provided excellent service and would be captured on the *positive* sub-branch while the suppliers, who underperformed would be put on the *negative* sub-branch. Depending on team maturity, the Project Manager could also include a branch on himself/herself allowing the team to comment on what he did well and what could have been better.

The project manager should circulate amongst the project team the Mind Map template on learnings as shown in fig 7.2 much in advance of the closure meet to allow each member identify the elements, which they felt went well and what could be improved.

(ii) *Closure Meet:* The closure meet can be a difficult meeting if the pre-work - as indicated in the previous section - is not done. The preferred sequence to go about the meet would be as follows:

a) *Project Summary*: The Project Manager summarizes the project, highlighting the achievements and appreciating the team for their efforts.

b) *Pending Items checklist*: The pending items Mind Map is presented by the project manager to the team, taking more inputs, where necessary, on the Mind Map.

c) *Collecting the learnings*: This represents the heart of the closure meet. Group Collaboration is essential for sharing learnings in a fun and in an engaging manner. A Mind Map is an excellent tool for such collaboration with others to harness the response of all members of the group in a dynamic and creative way. This becomes even easier when every individual is ready with his learnings using the Mind Map template as discussed in the previous section. For smaller project teams of 4 to 6 members, the manager could begin directly by taking individual inputs on every aspect to generate a single consolidated Mind Map in the meeting itself. For bigger teams, it would be preferable to break into smaller groups of 3 to 4 members allowing them to combine the learnings into a single Mind Map and then later make one final summary map collating the inputs from the individual teams. The Project Manager could either use the whiteboard for the Mind Map or any of the Mind Mapping software for the purpose.

d) *Identifying actions*: Once all the learnings are visible, determine three biggest pain points amongst all the identified negatives are impacting the customer, team or the project team's management. These are translated into actions, which preferably during the meet itself, the project manager must assign to individuals with timelines.

e) *Closure*: Finally, the Project Manager closes the meet summarizing the key achievements, learnings and actions arising from this valuable meet. He should end the meet with a thanks to the team announcing the date for celebrating the team's success.

(iii) *Post meet activities:* The post meet activities involve circulating amongst the relevant stakeholders the final project pendency Mind Map, the learnings Mind Map and the three most important actions to be taken.

Once through with each of these phases, the Project team is ready for reassignment enriched with the learnings from the last project.

USING MIND MAPS FOR RETROSPECTIVE MEETS IN AGILE PM PRACTICE

As discussed earlier, the Agile practices for Project Management deliver the project work in incremental parts with each time boxed development cycle called a sprint. The Agile method prescribes a Retrospective Meet

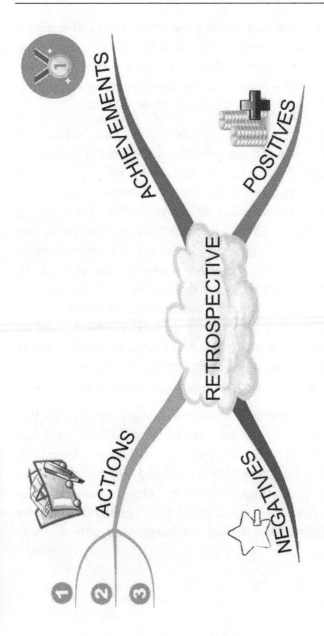

Figure 7.3: Mind Map for conducting effective Retrospective Meets

at the end of each sprint cycle. This retrospective meet is like a mini closing meet and focuses on continuous improvement over subsequent sprint cycles. A simple but powerful Mind Map as shown in figure 7.3 helps in enhancing the effectiveness of retrospectives.

The first branch of the Mind Map focuses on achievement or the progress made during the sprint. The actual work done in the sprint is noted purely from a factual perspective on the sub-branches. The second main branch captures what went well in the sprint or the positives. The third branch looks at what could have been done better or the scope for improvement. The last branch, viz, what represents the crux of the meeting, identifies at most three action points based on the improvement points highlighted and related discussion in the meeting. Similar to the visual dashboard used for tracking work packets to completion, this Mind Map can easily be maintained as a retrospective dashboard doing away with the need of circulating minutes post the meet.

Any experienced project manager will confess that project closure is not purely a left brained or linear activity but has to deal a lot more with the emotional side of an individual and the team. Mind Maps are the perfect whole brain thinking tools for group collaboration as these enable synergistic interaction, igniting the collective intelligence and letting the team work with a group attitude while tapping the uniqueness of every member.

CHAPTER 8

Organizational Deployment of Mind Maps

"In order to properly understand the big picture, everyone should fear becoming mentally clouded and obsessed with one small section of truth" - *Xun Zi*

We have seen a number of ways in this book how Mind Maps can be used during the complete lifecycle of the Project. So, the next logical question is how do we institutionalize this kind of thinking at the organizational level? We will take a look at the broad steps in this regard but before let's touch upon another subject, *"Project Portfolio Management"*--- an important topic from the point of view of both CXOs and the Project Management Office (PMO). A good alignment between projects and the organization's strategic objectives is a must for the organization's long term profitability.

Mind Maps for Project Portfolio Management

So what is Project Portfolio Management? Let's understand this with a simple analogy. The orchestra conductor is the Portfolio Manager responsible for the final symphony being produced by his band wherein each member plays his/her individual instrument. The final symphony is achieved only when everyone individually follows the "notes" of the orchestra conductor. In a similar fashion, Project Portfolio Management allows organizations to thrive by utilizing tools, which help integrate data from individual programs and/or projects. (Program is a collection of Projects with some commonality in them either in intent or nature of product)

So a key element of a good project portfolio management would be the clarity it conveys in the big picture when all the projects are put together. Given their inherent strength to stitch diverse information together, Mind Maps serve as a valuable tool for managing a project portfolio as it easily allows for capturing the satellite view along with the interconnections, if any, between the projects.

The important point then to be addressed in portfolio management is how to group the projects so that they enable important decisions by the executive leadership team. The key decisions or insights that the top management would be interested in while reviewing a portfolio are as follows:

a) Are all the projects aligned to the current bigger strategic objective of the organization?

b) Which are the most important and critical projects?

c) Are there any issues to be addressed in the top priority projects?

d) Are there any projects that need to be aborted?

e) Which are the projects, which are consuming the maximum resources? Is this justified?

Any tool, which can assist answering the above questions, makes for a good candidate for managing project portfolios.

Project grouping can be driven by variety of factors for portfolio analysis depending on the final intent thereby resulting in different ways of project stratification. So your project grouping could be led by ROI, Strategic Business Units, Markets, Costs, Customer or simply by the Project Lifecycle.

Let's build a Mind Map by grouping projects by their lifecycle, which would adequately demonstrate the usefulness of Mind Maps. We have looked at Mind Mapping opportunities at *Project Initiation, Execution* and *Closing* in this book. We could do a project portfolio analysis using these phases as shown in Figure 8.1.

The first three branches of the project capture each of the three project phases, namely, *Initiation, Execution* and *Closing*. Additionally, there is a fourth branch - *Stalled* - which is used to capture projects *Stalled* due to a variety of reasons before they reach their end goals.

The various projects in an organization (or a division) can be mapped easily onto this Mind Map. All projects, which are about to commence or are in the pipeline, are put on the sub-branches of the *Initiation* main branch. Similarly, projects in execution and those in the closing phase are mapped on the *Execution* and *Closing* sub-branches respectively. And as indicated earlier, stalled projects are parked on the last branch *Stalled*.

Sub-branches arising out of each of the project on the Mind Map should contain top level important metrics

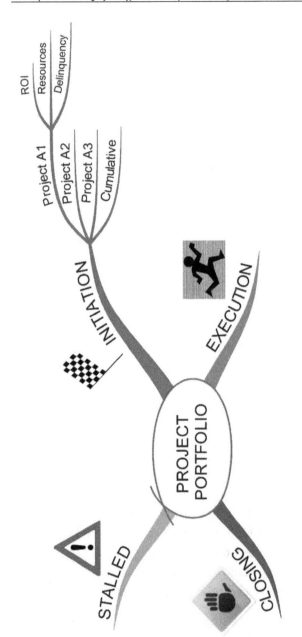

Figure 8.1: *Project Portfolio Management using Mind Maps*

such as ROI, Resources consumed, Delinquency etc. It is essential that we have at least one metric, which helps determine strategic alignment with the organization's bigger goals. The most important project(s) in each of the branches can also be highlighted. Besides all the project branches, an additional sub-branch can also be used for capturing the cumulative metric by project phases.

Connections or relations between multiple projects can be indicated by dotted lines. A main branch of the Mind Map can also be used to identify issues, which one may want to present to the senior management.

The advantage of this kind of a Map is that, firstly, it is easy to make, secondly, the Mind Map software allows for presentation of this Mind Map in slices easily understood by the audience, and finally, it helps answer most of the questions or insights necessary for the top management to take decisions, as may be necessary.

Similar Mind Maps can be made using a different stratification (as against project phases), such as by Customer, ROI etc., as had been indicated earlier. The key is to understand the intent or the organizational mission and then slice the project data accordingly to showcase compliance to the overall strategy as also issues to be addressed.

There are a number of opportunities that have been showcased in this book for using Mind Maps at an individual project level as well as management of project portfolios at an organizational level. Any PMO in an organization, serious about introducing Mind Maps in their projects, would need to do this in a step by step fashion. The next section outlines steps the PMO should take to deploy, and derive benefit, from Mind Mapping.

Suggestions for PMO to deploy Mind Maps in their organization

There are various types of PMO models being used by organizations ranging from the purely Supporting PMO (which primarily operates in an advisory/consulting mode) to Directive PMO (which has full control on the project and the resources).

Irrespective of the PMO model, there are certain steps that the PMO can take to deploy Mind Maps for Project Management in their organization. These are outlined below.

1. *Mind Map training sessions.* Begin with a Mind Map Training session for the complete PMO along with key project managers, who the PMO feels would be open to change and experimenting with something as new as Mind Maps. The training session is most effective when it covers not only an introduction to Mind Mapping but also its practical usage for issues specific to an Organization/Project Management. This is important since Mind Maps are a radically different way to work and need to be given time before you can experience success using this tool.

2. *Identify a Pilot Project team.* Subsequent to the training session, seek volunteer Project Managers eager to experiment with Mind Maps in their teams.

3. *Brainstorm.* Do a quick brainstorming using Mind Maps with this Project team to identify possible areas for improving their Project Management maturity.

4. *Identify Mind Mapping Opportunities.* Let's say one of the weakness identified by the team is *Communication Management.* Look at how Mind Maps (as detailed in Chapter 4) can help in building a good Project *Communication Plan* and begin implementing the same.

5. *Periodic Feedbacks.* The PMO should then take regular feedback from the team and support them in their new journey, gradually identifying more areas for using and deriving benefits from Mind Maps.

6. *Spread the good word* The Project team and the PMO should use every opportunity to spread and share the success story with other teams as well as get more teams to participate.

7. *Institutionalize the practice.* Once a few project teams start experiencing success using Mind Maps, this should give sufficient confidence to the PMO to institutionalize the practice as may be best suited for the organization. This could be approached either by Project Lifecycles (for example, maximizing Mind Map usage for Project feasibility and Initiation) or by specific areas such as Risk Management, Communication Management etc.

The steps elucidated above are broad guidelines and would require to be tweaked basis realities unique to every organization.

Project Portfolio Management and PMO are important tools for any organization serious about enhancing their Project Management maturity. And Mind Maps have the potential to make them even more effective and efficient.

Chapter 9

Key Messages and The Way Forward

"To raise new questions, new possibilities, to regard old problems from a new angle, requires creative imagination and marks real advance in science"
                                                    – Albert Einstein

The world around us is changing at a rapid pace with new products and services. There is no reason to believe that at any time soon humanity will be relieved of its tasks of managing projects. What would and needs to change is the way organizations manage projects. Project Management practices need to undergo a tectonic shift and this shift is already visible with the introduction of some modern project management methodologies like Agile.

Project management is both an art and a science requiring our both left and right cortical skills. The multitude of tools for PM, however, that we find in the market seem to focus strongly on logic and measurements that have in effect a left brain dominance. Mind Maps is the perfect approach to fill in this missing gap and take Project Management to its next level of maturity where it becomes more engaging resulting in more successful projects. Mind Maps are flexible, natural and most of all,

ʼning of our brain, and are hence the
ʻor Project Management discipline for
ʼe project manager's journey across
ⱼycle.

ⱼgressively the projects are going to become
ⱼncreasingly complex, more importantly, interdependent on a variety of factors; will have more unknowns to start with and eventually would need to cater to the requirements of a green sustainable world. The triple constraint of Time, Cost & Quality would, however, still be valid. In this kind of environment, simple techniques like Mind Maps would help breathe fresh life into traditional project management techniques filling in the gap for the much needed creativity for managing projects.

There are some key messages that emerge from this book, which are presented below:

Chapter 1: Project Management-Mind Maps: The Perfect Marriage!

A new definition is the need of the hour for a "project", which demands greater creativity from the project team and all stakeholders.

Innovation over the years has been an attempt of the human civilization to mimic the working of the human body itself in the external and on a bigger scale.

Managing Projects is not purely a left brain activity but a holistic approach to create something new and unique.

Chapter 2: Frameworks for Project Management and Mind Mapping

Introduction of Project Management methodologies like Agile have unconsciously introduced elements of holistic brain thinking and at the same time reducing left brain aspects like relying too much on documents and structures.

Mind Mapping clearly encourages whole brain thinking, making it the perfect tool for taking project management to the next level.

Chapter 3: The Subtle "Nature" in Project Management and Mind Maps

Creation in nature is the most outstanding Project Management in action. The life cycle of a Project is similar to the life cycle of a human journey from cradle to grave.

Mind Maps are visible everywhere in nature, beginning with the Big Bang and reflected in every "flower" of creation, including the human brain.

Chapter 4: Key Project Management Skills and How Mind Maps can magnify them

Independent of the project type or industry, there is a set of skills, which are a must for every project manager and which include Leading, Communicating, Negotiation, Problem Solving, Influencing the organization, an Attitude of Learning and Improvement, a Sense of Urgency and an Ability to embrace Ambiguity. And the good news is that Mind Maps are easily applied in all these areas with immediate gains.

Chapter 5: The Birth: Initiation or Project Start

The start of a project is similar in characteristic to a new born baby. The project idea is new, creates excitement, is full of potential but at the same time needs protection. The important aspects of a project at start are: Feasibility Check, Project Charter, Scope Definition, Planning, Communication and Risk and Opportunities Management. Multiple opportunities exist in each of these areas for gainfully applying Mind Maps.

Chapter 6: The Busy Life: Project Execution

The execution phase of a project is the bridge between nebulous thoughts at the start of the project with the end of the project i.e. the final tangible product or service. The aspects of Project Management most important at this point of time are Managing Relations and Communications, Managing Scope, Time Management, Cost Management, Quality Management, Risk and Opportunities Management, and finally Procurement Management. Each of these areas again presents innumerable opportunities for using Mind Maps to enhance the probability of project success.

Chapter 7: The Project End: Doorway to a new beginning

The closing phase is similar to our sunset years. The rate of consumption of resources is low and it is a time for reflection on the learnings from the project, irrespective of the final project outcome. Mind Mapping is an extremely effective tool for conducting formal closure meets and generating ideas for continuous improvement in the future.

Chapter 8: Organizational Deployment of Mind Maps

In the last chapter we saw how Mind Maps can be used for Project Portfolio Management and more importantly how an organization can gradually institutionalize a culture of Mind Mapping for managing projects. So we discussed how we can start with an awareness training followed by a pilot which can be then be used to scale up the deployment of Mind Maps in an organization.

A number of Mind Mapping examples are available in this book. These Mind Maps are best used as templates or draft guidance for anyone to start experimenting in various projects. The idea is not to adopt all the Mind Maps highlighted here but to start experimenting with Mind Maps, which are most appealing for your project. You may develop an addiction to this wonderful tool and kick start your journey of creativity, discovering your brain's full potential.

Ever since man's existence on this planet, Mind Maps have been were physically existent in every individual's brain in the form of a neural network. With the evolution of man, this network or these Mind Maps inside the brain started becoming more complex leading to enhanced creativity, hence more creation and more projects as time progressed! Though somewhere along history, we began relying heavily on linear thinking, there were still geniuses like Leonardo Da Vinci, who could combine rational and intuitive thinking in the right degree to produce inventions far ahead of their times. And as indicated earlier in the book, such geniuses had a unique way of taking notes: rich in images or imagination and association. These giants were unconsciously "mapping" their thought in the physical world the way their brain was thinking internally. Through extensive brain research, Mr. Tony Buzan, the inventor of Mind Maps, has been able to identify laws of Mind Mapping, which very closely reflect the natural working of the brain. Thanks to his efforts, more and more schools, colleges and institutes have started adopting Mind Maps as the new age teaching and learning tool. Mr. Tony Buzan rightly calls this a "Genius Tool", which allows anyone to tap into their uniqueness and apply it with ease to the subject at hand.

A project facilitates creation, a Mind Map allows creativity to flow; a project provides vision, a Mind Map enhances the engagement towards vision achievement; a project is identified with "work", a Mind Map with "engagement"; a project allows for a unique creation, a Mind Map brings out your uniqueness; and finally while a project has boundaries, the only boundaries that a Mind Map has are the shores of your thoughts. Thus a synergy of these subjects results in an unbounded creativity in creation.

It is the simplicity of an approach that determines its universal appeal for adoption of a new technique across industries and sectors. Mind Maps possess and exhibit that simplicity, working at the fundamental thought level thereby enhancing one's thinking process. It's application is limited only by our imagination. And imagination is nothing but our thoughts getting associated in a way unique with us. Mind Maps help us precisely express this internal process.

Beyond atoms and molecules, we build ourselves everyday with our thoughts and imagination. Let's use Mind Maps to sharpen ourselves from inside out!

About the Author

After two decades of rich industry experience, Maneesh has embarked on a journey to pursue his passion for Mind Mapping and Project Management. He has set up his firm (www.maneeshdutt.com) to enable Ideas, Innovation and Individuals to allow organizations to enhance their efficiency and effectiveness. A passionate and die-hard fan of Mind

Maneesh Dutt

Maps, these form the backbone of all his workshops. He has made it his mission to take Mind Maps to all corners of India covering organizations and academia, including schools and colleges.

He is an engineer from IIT Delhi and MBA by education. A ThinkBuzan Licensed Instructor (TLI) for Mind Maps, he has been trained by the inventor of Mind Maps himself, Mr. Tony Buzan.

Maneesh is a Project Management Professional (PMP) from the Project Management Institute and a Certified Scrum Trainer for Agile Scrum Practices. He has conducted numerous training sessions on Project Management, Mind Mapping and Innovation, many of these for corporate clients across industry. His commitment to delivering outstanding training programs is apparent from the excellent ratings and feedbacks he has received for all his sessions.

Bibliography

[1] T. Buzan, How To Mind Map, London: Thorsons, 2002.

[2] C. Griffiths and M. Costi, GRASP the Solution, UK: Proactive Press, 2011.

[3] PMI, A Guide to the Project Management Body of Knowledge, Pennsylvania: Project Management Institute, 2013.

[4] McKinsey & Company, University of Oxford, "Study On Large scale IT Projects," October 2012.

[5] E. G. Carayannis,, Y. H. Kwak and F. T. Anbari, Brief History of Project Management, Quorum Books, 2003.

[6] M. E. Moreira, M. Lester and S. Holzner, Agile for dummies, Indianapolic, Indiana: Wiley Publishing Inc., 2011.

[7] Ricardo Hausmann, Harvard University; Laura D. Tyson, University of California, Berkeley; Saadia Zahidi, World Economic Forum, "The Global Gender Gap Report," World Economic Forum, Geneva, Switzerland, 2012.

[8] M. J. Gelb, How to Think Like Leonardo da Vinci, London: HarperElement, 2009.

[9] K. Lawrence, "Developing Leaders in a VUCA world," UNC Kenan-Flagler Business School, 2013.

[10]   T. Buzan and C. Griffiths, Mind Maps for Business, Great Britain: BBC Active, 2010.

[11]   T. Buzan and B. Buzan, The Mind Map Book, Great Britain: BBC Active, 2010.

[12]   M. Dutt, "Using Mind Maps to Enhance Creativity When Managing Projects," *ASQ Journal of Participation,* 2014.

[13]   T. Buzan, "Think Buzan," [Online]. Available: http://thinkbuzan.com/articles/mindmappingworks/.

[14]   A. J. Mento, P. Martinelli and J. R. M., "Mind Mapping in Executive Education: Applications and Outcomes," *The Journal of Management Development, Vol. 18, Issue 4.,* pp. 390-416, 1999.

[15]   R. Fisher and W. Ury, Getting to Yes, New York: Penguin Books, 1991.

[16]   A. Mueller, M. Johnston and D. Bligh, "Joining Mind Mapping And Care Planning to Enhance Student Critical Thinking and achieve holistic Nursing Care," *Nursing Diagnosis, 13,1,* p. Pg 24, 2002.

[17]   S. R. Covey, The Seven Habits of highly effective people, New York: Simon & Schuster, 1989.

[18]   M. Dutt and N. Kar, "The Project Managers Styles," *"Synergy" by PMI North India Chapter,* p. 3, April 2001, Issue 1.

[19]   S. Thomke, Managing Product and service Development: Text and Cases, Mcgraw Hill, 2007.

[20]   T. Chuan, M. K. Xie and X. X. Shen, "'Development of Innovative Products Using Kano's Model and Quality Function Deployment,'" *International Journal of Innovation Management,* pp. 271-286, 1999, Vol 3, No. 3.

[21]   J. Greene and A. Stellman, Head First PMP, Sebastopol, CA: O Reilly, July 2009.

Few Testimonials from Participant From Various Organisations Who Have Attended The Mind Map Workshops of The Author Maneesh Dutt

"Session was very good and by using this we can find solution to various problems. Mr. Maneesh is a very good presenter, he customized the presentation as per pharma industry and also designed the topic in a way to give maximum benefit to the participants"

– *Sandipan Roy,*
Sun Pharma

"The course content and the way of presentation was excellent. The exercises were quite good"

– Nirmal Kumar Parida,
Samsung

"Very Interesting!! Eye Opener!! Mind Opener!!"

– *Hemali Bhutani Mahajan,*
Genesis Burson Marsteller

"In one word: Brilliant!! Can be potentially life changing for an individual"

– *Sudeep B.,*
BioXcel Corporation

"Amazing! Engaging! Enhancing!"

> *– Vikas Chandwani,*
> *Trainer & Coach*

"Something new, innovative, creative, easily applicable concept to get clarity and direction in career and personal life"

> *– Shoumi Dasgupta,*
> **IBEF**

"Training was extremely commendable. All aspects which are necessary to transform oneself from good to great have been discussed"

> *– Dr. Sahab Singh, Faculty,*
> **Dronachrya Group of Institute**

"The session of Mind Map was fantastic, I learnt a lot of things. The trainer's knowledge was mind blowing"

> *– Priti Mishra, Student,*
> **Dronacharya Group of Institute**.

Amazing learning experience, discovered the magic of Mind Maps and the power to reach new possibilities. Content was very interesting and structure indeed engaging"

> *– Pawan Chabra,*
> **IBEF**

"It was a great learning as I was introduced to this wonderful concept for the first time in my life. Overall a great Experience"

> *– Rajesh Saluda,*
> **Lunawat & Co**.

"It's a new concept & can be utilized in every aspect of Life whether work or family & Friends"

– Anil Singh,
Olympus Medical Systems India Pvt. Ltd.

"After a long time new thing to learn which will definitely help to enhance my skills. A must have training session for everyone"

– Rahul Sharma,
Saigun Technologies Pvt. Ltd.

Great Concept, Great activities, exercises, Very Engaging Content. Can be practically applied to a lot of situations. Maneesh is very knowledgeable, engaged very well with everyone, was approachable, answered all questions very well & clearly explained concepts.

– Ratnabali Banerjee,
Innodata

"Maneesh has deep knowledge and simplified the hard points"

– Shailendra Hasabe,
Mahle Filter Systems

Book Reviews for the First Edition

"Just as the LEAN movement transformed the Manufacturing industry, Mind Maps can do the same to the field of Project Management. A Mind Map helps cuts across the noise in multiple situations, brings into focus the core issue and ignites creativity through whole brain thinking. Through this book Maneesh has provided a framework and examples to apply Mind Mapping to the practice of Project Management - a bold move that will encourage creative thinking and problem solving. A must read for organizational heads and all project managers."

– Nitin Kulkarni, Founder & Principal Consultant,
Elevo Consulting

"The book is a Project management and Mind Maps toolkit coming from a practicing professional and trainer Maneesh Dutt. It is a guide map for decision makers to enable project professionals become more creative and innovative in managing projects. Projects, today, are more like a hundred meter sprint than a marathon and deserve nimble techniques like Mind Maps to execute better. The book picks up the threads from project management fundamentals along with inspiration from nature and provides a rich array of Mind Map templates allowing organizations to kick start their journey towards better project management. A real boon to organizations that are involved in any Project activity!"

– Gaurang Joshipura, Managing Director,
Zeppelin Systems India Pvt. Ltd.

CPSIA information can be obtained
at www.ICGtesting.com
Printed in the USA
FSHW022052010120
65645FS